Participant Guide for the Beegle
If Not Me, Then Who? Empowering Our Neighbors

Dr. Donna M. Beegle
Copyright © 2017 by Donna M. Beegle, Ed.D.
First Printing August 2017
Printed in the United States of America
by Communication Across Barriers, Inc.
PO Box 23071, Tigard, OR 97281
All rights reserved.
ISBN # 978-1-934085-11-0

By: Dr. Donna Beegle
Editors: Debbie Ellis and Cory Jubitz
Design and layout: Wanda Buck of Lou Graphics, www.lougraphics.com

Communication Across Barriers
www.combarriers.com
(503) 590-4599

Copies of this book, the facilitator's guide, and DVD are available
at www.combarriers.com/ifnotme.

This Beegle Poverty Awareness Training is a production of Digital Laundry (www.digitallaundry.net) in partnership with St. Vincent de Paul (www.svdpusa.org).

Communication Across Barriers and Dr. Donna M. Beegle

After growing up in generational migrant labor poverty, leaving school for marriage at 15, having two children, and continuing to cope with poverty, Donna found herself, at 25, with no husband, little education, and no job skills. What followed—in 10 short years—were self-confidence, a G.E.D., an A.A. in journalism, a B.A. (with honors) in communication, an M.A. in communication with a minor in gender studies (with honors), and completion of an Ed.D. in educational leadership.

Donna M. Beegle, Ed.D., is an authentic voice who speaks, writes, and trains across the nation to break the iron cage of poverty. She brings unique insights from having grown up in the deepest poverty in America and from studying and speaking on poverty for over 25 years. She is the author of *See Poverty...Be the Difference, Breaking Poverty Barriers to Equal Justice*, and *An Action Approach to Educating Students in Poverty*. Donna's inspiring story and work have been featured in newspapers around the nation, on local TV, and on national channels such as PBS and CNN. Donna founded Communication Across Barriers, Inc., in 1990 with her mentor Dr. Bob Fulford.

Communication Across Barriers, Inc., is dedicated to broadening and improving opportunities for all people who live in the war zone of poverty.

Our far-reaching goals are to:

- Assist people living in the crisis of poverty to move out and stay out of poverty. We provide education and tools to remove the shame, rebuild the confidence and hope, reduce the isolation, and assist people in obtaining the education and skills needed to earn a living.

- Empower communities and organizations to "fight poverty, not the people who live in it." We illuminate real and structural causes of poverty and provide life-changing information that shatters common myths and stereotypes about people who live in poverty.

- Offer research-based strategies and insider perspectives for improving relationships, communication, and opportunities.

- Develop an army of speakers and trainers who can educate and assist organizations in becoming poverty informed.

- Provide models and step-by-step programs that increase a poverty-informed, community-wide approach to fighting poverty.

- Educate and engage people who are not in poverty with tools and avenues for making a difference in their own communities.

Table of Contents

	Page
Introduction	1
Case Study	2
Segment 1: Understanding Poverty	7
America's Knowledge of Poverty	7
Poverty Realities in America	8
Poverty Myths	12
Attitudes and Beliefs	15
Segment 2: Insider's Perspective	17
Why an Insider's Perspective?	17
Excerpt from the Donna M. Beegle Story	18
What Efforts Made the Most Difference? Strategies to Break Poverty Barriers	24
Practical Tips	27
Segment 3: What Does the Word Poverty Mean?	29
Federal Poverty Guidelines	29
Context of Poverty	30
Poverty Crosses Race	34
Segment 4: Understanding the Perspectives of People in Poverty	36
Social Class Context Shapes Worldview	36
The Worldview Taught by Poverty	37
Identification—A Key Ingredient to Building Common Ground with Your Neighbors in Poverty	38
Segment 5: Tools for Improving Communication and Relationships	41
Building Relationships and Navigating—Practical Ways to Build Trust and Relationships That Matter	41
Oral and Print—Two Distinct Communication and Learning Styles	43
10 Strategies to Communicate and Build Relationships That Matter	51
Segment 6: Call to Action, Call to Hope	54
What Can You Do?	55
Strategies to Remove Shame	56
Strategies to Rebuild Hope	57
Strategies to Reduce Isolation	57
Strategies for Creating a Poverty-Informed Community	58
Segment 7: Digging Deeper	61
Systemic Change	61
Single-Focus Approach	62
The Opportunity Community Model	63
Next Steps	67

List of Activities   Page

Pre-Training Reflection 6

There Is Enough 10

Segment 1: Case Study 16

Segment 2: Case Study 28

Segment 3: Case Study 35

Segment 4: Case Study 40

What Is Your Dominant Communication Style? 49

Segment 5: Case Study 53

Segment 6: Case Study 60

Segment 7: Case Study 66

Post-Training Reflection 70

Introduction

We want to express our sincere gratitude for your desire and willingness to make a difference for your Neighbors who live in the crisis of poverty. Dr. Donna M. Beegle and the Communication Across Barriers (CAB) team have worked extensively to prepare this poverty awareness training that will assist you to go beyond addressing immediate needs (such as providing food boxes, temporary shelter, and financial assistance with rent and utilities) to a more systemic approach for helping your Neighbors to move out and stay out of the crisis of poverty.

The goal of this poverty awareness training is to provide a deeper understanding of the many different life experiences of poverty along with best practices and tools for improving outcomes. The information gained in this training includes poverty competency tools for improving communication and relationships, as well as strategies for planning and creating systemic change.

Because of this training, you will be able to:

- Name and describe some lived experiences of poverty and how each impacts your Neighbors
- Discuss how poverty affects worldview, relationships, communication, and learning
- Better understand how people who are living in the crisis of poverty experience helping professionals and volunteers
- Describe how and where most Americans get their knowledge of people living in poverty and how that affects our efforts to break barriers
- Develop skills for identifying and overcoming unconscious bias that can get in the way of empowering people living in poverty
- Gain communication strategies for building trust and relationships that assist in breaking poverty barriers
- Obtain tools for working with community partners to provide a comprehensive, poverty-informed approach that empowers our Neighbors

This training will challenge you to reflect deeply on what you believe about poverty and the people who live in it—examining how your perspectives impact the ways you communicate and relate with those you wish to empower. It will also provide proven strategies and practical action steps for improving outcomes for your Neighbors who are living in the crisis of poverty. By the end of this Beegle poverty awareness training, you will see how you can use existing resources to change lives.

CASE STUDY

The family story below is based on real-life experiences of poverty. It is not a depiction of one family, but rather a compilation of several families to add depth to the story and portray the complexity of the nature of poverty. Please get acquainted with Jeffrey and Colleen. Think about their story as you view the training videos and go through the activities in the guidebook. Their story will be used for you to reflect upon and act out in various role play/case study scenarios as we progress through this learning guide.

Jeffrey and Colleen

Jeffrey and Colleen grew up in Georgia in working-class neighborhoods. Neither of Jeffrey's parents graduated from high school. They dropped out in their sophomore and junior years of high school to go to work and help support their families. His parents married before they were 18 years old. Because of a learning disability, Colleen's mom graduated from high school with a modified diploma. Colleen's dad dropped out when he was a junior. He had been held back a grade in elementary school, so he felt much older than his peers and was unable to connect and relate with them. When the chance came to join the Army, he dropped out, got his GED, and enlisted. When he returned from his service, he married his high school sweetheart...Colleen's mom. Due to their limited education and marketable skills, both sets of their parents worked but barely made enough money to make ends meet.

Jeffrey and Colleen met and fell in love during high school. Jeffrey was two years older than Colleen. At the beginning of his senior year, Colleen learned she was pregnant. They celebrated their good fortune and planned a small family wedding around their Christmas break. After the wedding, Jeffrey continued to go to school and graduated with his class. But because of the morning sickness, changes in her body, and complications of her pregnancy, Colleen dropped out during the winter break—just after the first term of her sophomore year. Their first son was born shortly before Jeffrey's graduation.

While Jeffrey finished school, he and Colleen lived with his parents in a rented one-bedroom house. Jeffrey, Colleen, and the baby slept in what was supposed to be the laundry room. Since the family did not have a washer or dryer, they put a mattress on the floor and it became their bedroom. Jeffrey's grandma slept on the couch.

Jeffrey and Colleen desperately wanted their own place. When Jeffrey was hired at a local warehouse, they were ecstatic. A couple of months after Jeffrey started work, they moved into a small, run-down rental home on the outskirts of town. Jeffrey was not afraid of a "run-down" home because he had learned a lot of tips and tricks for fixing lots of things from his family. So, he worked with his dads and uncles to fix a lot of the issues within the house. Colleen had a great eye and was able to creatively decorate her home with finds from thrift stores and garage sales.

While working and raising a family and keeping house was often daunting, Jeffrey and Colleen loved the new life they were building and the family they were creating. Not long after the birth of their son, Colleen became pregnant with twins, a boy and a girl. Even though Colleen had a limited formal education, she discovered she had some great talents for teaching her kids and devoted her time to making sure they were learning and growing up healthy. Her dream was that each of her three children would finish high school, since she never got to. Jeffrey was a hands-on dad who loved teaching the children how to carve wood into bears, tigers, and other animals. This was a skill that he had learned from his Native American family members on his mom's side of the family. Everyone raved about the pieces he created.

Because Jeffrey only had a high school education, he struggled to move up in the company. They wanted someone with more skills than he had. Although Jeffrey was a good worker, raises were minimal and promotions almost nonexistent. The only people moving up in the company were those who were more educated and skilled.

Jeffrey's work at the warehouse was fairly consistent, but at times his hours were cut to part-time. His part-time hours were always 27 hours a week or less so that his employer was not required to pay for his medical insurance. His take-home pay was just less than $1,200 a month.

Jeffrey was occasionally able to pick up extra money from working a few hours at a local tire shop. The hours were not stable and the money was paid "under the table." Even though he worked two jobs, Jeffrey and his family lived paycheck to paycheck. Jeffrey dreamed of being able to quit the two jobs and have his own business carving wood products.

Because Colleen lacked a high school diploma and because the cost of daycare would take every penny of any potential paycheck she could make, Colleen was a stay-at-home mom. She supplemented the family income by growing a garden, raising chickens for eggs, and selling handmade items at bazaars and thrift stores.

During the times that Jeffrey was working part-time, there was no savings on which to live, which caused Colleen and Jeffrey to rely on social services—often getting assistance through the Supplemental Nutrition Assistance Program (SNAP—formerly known as food stamps) and temporary assistance with rent and utilities. Often, Colleen would have to tell agencies that Jeffrey had left her, because his part-time income put them over the limit for getting the help they desperately needed. All of this made Jeffrey feel inadequate as a husband and father. During those times, he would grow quiet and depressed and angered easily.

During one of these down times, shortly before their 10th anniversary, Jeffrey and Colleen were awakened by the smell of smoke. Colleen ran to her daughter's room while Jeffrey got the boys out of the house. The fire had started in the old wiring in the wall between their daughter's bedroom and the garage. She suffered a lot of smoke inhalation and was unconscious when Colleen came into her room. She had to carry her from the home.

Before the fire department was able to get to the house, it was engulfed in flames. After medical treatment for smoke inhalation and minor burns, the family was released from the hospital and returned to their home to find any possessions that might be saved.

While walking through the rubble, they found nothing to take with them. They had lost all the possessions that they had acquired over their married life. They lost all the photos of their courtship and wedding, and all the pictures of their children's births and the events throughout their young lives. They lost all the important paperwork that chronicled their life together—wedding certificate, birth certificates, school records, and Jeffrey's high school diploma. They lost all the items that had been given to them from family members. They lost their Christmas decorations and all the presents that they had purchased for their kids. And, because the fire started in the garage, they lost their only vehicle. They were alive and well...but had lost everything.

Because it was a downtime at the factory, they had not paid their car and renters insurance. Nothing would be covered. Red Cross stepped in and assisted the family with a three-month motel voucher. They also signed the family up for a "giving tree" so that the family would have some presents and a nice meal for Christmas. Using public transportation, they searched for a place to live and did their best to get their children to school and appointments.

Because Jeffrey's take-home pay at the time was just less than $1,200 a month, it was difficult to find a new place to live. Frustration and depression mounted when they realized the average monthly rent for a one-bedroom was $750. They could pay that, but not the first, last, and deposits the landlords were requiring. Paying the application fee of $45 per person every time they applied was also eating up the little cash they had. In addition, they were having difficulty finding something appropriate near the kids' schools and Jeffrey's job. Jeffrey put in applications at several places for a second job, but no one was calling. Colleen called St. Vincent de Paul to ask for help.

Pre-Training Reflection

Before the training, please take a few minutes to reflect on the following questions and write down your answers as completely and thoughtfully as possible.

1. *When you hear the word poverty, what are the first images and words that come to your mind?*

2. *What do you believe causes poverty?*

3. *Where do your beliefs about poverty come from?*

4. *What needs to be done to eradicate poverty? List at least two actions that need to be taken to break poverty barriers.*

5. *Based on your past interactions with your Neighbors in poverty, how were your experiences and exposure to opportunities—while growing up—similar to or different from those of the people struggling in poverty whom you want to empower?*

Segment 1: Understanding Poverty

> **Guiding Questions**
> - Where do most people get their information about poverty?
> - What myths and stereotypes prevent us from breaking poverty barriers?
> - How do our own attitudes and beliefs about poverty shape our actions?

America's Knowledge of Poverty

Can you guess where most people learn about poverty and its impacts on our Neighbors? Many believe it is from our colleges and universities, but in fact, the number-one teacher of poverty in America is the media! We graduate people from college to serve as professionals in health, social service, faith-based organizations, education, business, and as elected officials without a fundamental understanding of poverty—leaving the media as the number-one source for information on what poverty means, its causes, and potential solutions. Most would agree that the media tends to dramatize, sensationalize, and present extreme cases—resulting in deeply embedded stereotypes of poverty in our society.

Some people may learn about poverty from a life experience and assume that their experience is the same as that of others facing poverty. Others often form perceptions about poverty from knowing a family or person who lives in poverty. That family or person becomes representative of all poverty experiences. Different life experiences of poverty and the facts about the real causes of and solutions to poverty are rarely presented. Therefore, most people remain unaware of the daily realities of poverty, even in their own communities.

In this country, we do an inadequate job of teaching people about poverty. Few professionals have had the course "The History of Poverty in the United States." Most Americans do not know the history or how we came to our current ideas on poverty. Few understand the models and approaches that have been used to address poverty. Even professionals who work with people in poverty graduate from college without ever having had a course on structural causes of poverty and how they impact our fellow human beings. Many people do not even know their state's minimum wage. If we do not know the minimum wage or what people on welfare are subsisting on, it is easy to fall into judgment. If we are judging, we cannot connect. If we cannot connect, we cannot communicate. If we cannot communicate, it will be difficult to understand their situations and work together to remove poverty obstacles.

The implications of this lack of poverty education are devastating. It fosters stereotypes with the general public and creates leaders and decision-makers who have little or no real understanding of poverty or the perspectives of people impacted by it. Ignorance about real poverty causes and their impacts often results in programs, policies, and procedures that are not only failing to move people out of poverty but—far too often—punish people for poverty conditions.

Poverty Realities in America

The Numbers **Far too many people, mostly children, suffer from poverty conditions**. In 2015, 13.5 percent of the population, 43.1 million Americans, lived in poverty (U.S. Census Bureau, 2016). Of that 43.1 million, about 14.5 million are children—19.7 percent of all children—living in families with incomes below the federal poverty threshold. Research shows that, on average, families need an income of about twice that level to cover basic expenses. Using this standard, 42 percent of children live in low-income families.

Housing One in four working households in America (10.6 million families) spends more than half of their pre-tax income on housing. This is a level that experts say is unhealthy, if not impossible, to sustain. In February 2016, the National Low Income Housing Coalition conducted a study that examined the cost of housing across the United States and found that there is no community in America where minimum-wage earners could reasonably afford to pay rent. In 86 percent of counties surveyed, even those who earned twice the minimum wage still did not earn enough money to pay rent and provide for their basic needs.

Welfare **Government assistance is disjointed and falls short of covering basic needs**. Less than 2 percent of the federal budget is allocated for welfare—now known as Temporary Assistance to Needy Families (TANF). Nationally, the average TANF check for one parent and two children is $478 per month. Twenty years ago, it was $408. In addition to the TANF check only increasing by $70 in the last 20 years, the percentages of households that actually receive funding has reduced significantely. According to the Center on Budget and Policy Priorities (2015), in 1997, 82 percent of those who qualified for Aid to Families with Dependent Children (the predecessor of TANF) received funds. New policies have made it more difficult for people in poverty to access

TANF. Thus, in 2012, only 23 percent of those who qualified actually received funds. In addition, TANF is no longer the largest anti-poverty intiative in the U.S. It has been largely replaced by the Earned Income Tax Credit (EITC). This tax credit is tied to work and provides subsidies (in the form of tax credits) to low-income wage earners. For those in deepest poverty, they seldom do their taxes and often, when able to find work, are paid under the table. Thus, this credit provides them with no relief.

Additionally, when a baby is born into a family already on welfare, 23 states add no cash to their monthly allotments. The few states that still provide additional support for the newborn, provide only $60 per month for the baby's care. For our neighbors who are disabled, the average check they receive is $756. Even though these funds barely cover basic needs, many people cling to them because they see no hope for earning money for survival with their housing instability; lack of access to transporation and childcare; and limited skills, education, and literacy levels.

Food **The rates of hunger in America continue to be extremely high for an industrialized nation**. In the United States, 46 million people suffer food insecurity, while one-third of this group experiences chronic hunger. A person on SNAP (food stamps) receives $1.89 per meal. In America, many people think hunger does not exist because of obesity. In reality, many in poverty face obesity issues because the food they can afford is full of carbohydrates and processed sugars. Healthy food is expensive.

Working Hard **Many people work hard and are still not making it**. There is a dominant belief in our society that if one works hard enough, they will do well. According to the recent census, two-thirds of people living in poverty are working 1.7 jobs and they cannot afford their rent. Even with two full-time minimum-wage incomes, the family is still under the Federal Poverty Guideline. Minimum wage is not a living wage!

Education **Youth living in poverty are the least likely to become educated in our nation**. Many students living in poverty have low academic achievement and schools struggle to address their needs. Families living in poverty often experience education as "stress" and see it as a place where they don't belong. A college education can help people break the barriers of poverty and escape its hardships, yet today, it is less likely a person in poverty will attain a college education than it was in the 1940s. For students from poverty who do make it to college, only 11 percent leave with a degree. Most drop out due to poverty impacts (no place to live and no money for utilities, food, and other basic needs).

Mentoring and Navigating Studies show that 59 percent of youth and adults in poverty have never had a mentor from a middle-class background. More than half of those living in poverty grow up without any meaningful connection to someone who understands how to navigate middle-class systems.

Effects of Poverty Many people in poverty have come to believe that something is wrong with them. They often internalize poverty as a personal deficiency and lose hope. They see no options for anything beyond an insufficient welfare/disability check or underground activities that barely pay enough to keep food on the table and often result in incarceration. Nearly 80 percent of people in prison cannot read at an eighth-grade level. A startling 50 percent of those in cages have untreated mental health struggles. Poverty affects educational success, health, and relationships, but mostly it affects the ability for humans to develop to their full potential.

We can do better! A deeper understanding of poverty and the barriers it presents is highly needed. It requires community members and professionals being consistent in saying, "Poverty is not okay and we are going to work to remove the barriers." It requires each and every one of us exploring what is in our hands to make a difference for those living in poverty. If we do not have the resources or skills to remove poverty barriers, we must build a resource and opportunity network and explore who might be able to assist us in removing the obstacles that prevent people from moving out of poverty.

There Is Enough: For the following multiple-choice questions, please circle the correct answers.

1. What was spent on pets for Valentine's Day 2016?		
$1 Million	$815 Million	$10 Million
2. What was spent on Hannah Montana, High School Musical, and Disney Princess merchandise in the height of the recession?		
$20 Million	$12 Billion	$26 Billion
3. What was the amount spent in October 2016 on Halloween (costumes and candy)?		
$1 Million	$8.4 Billion	$80 Million
4. How much money was spent on video games in one month last year?		
$1.5 Billion	$35 Million	$25.3 Billion
5. How much was spent on the Super Bowl in one weekend (in the U.S.)?		
$14.31 Billion	$27.25 Billion	$97.89 Million
6. What is the average spent on a person for one year in prison?		
$9,000	$18,000	$44,000

After discussing the answers to the quiz above, you will see that America is not a nation of scarcity. There are enough resources in both the public and private sectors to ensure that everyone has genuine opportunities to reach their fullest potential. There is enough land for everyone to have a place to lay their head. There is enough food, so no one should be hungry. Taxpayers spend a lot of money on the symptoms of poverty (e.g., paying for prisons, foster care, emergency rooms, and other poverty impacts). When we are poverty informed, we invest in our children and families to ensure everyone has authentic opportunities to develop to their fullest potential and give back to our communities.

A new paradigm:

1. A deeper understanding of poverty and its impacts on our Neighbors
2. A strengths perspective, stand in awe
3. A NASA attitude: Failure is not an option
4. Stronger partnerships

Poverty Myths

> *Myth:* **People in poverty don't want to work. They are lazy, unmotivated, and not smart.**

Fact: People in poverty do not have weaker work ethics or lower levels of motivation than wealthier people. Although people in poverty are often stereotyped as lazy, two-thirds of them work an average of 1.7 jobs; 83 percent of children from low-income families have at least one employed parent; and close to 60 percent of children have at least one parent who works full-time and year-round. According to the Economic Policy Institute, working adults who live in the crisis of poverty spend more hours working each week than their wealthier counterparts. In addition, they get jobs that demand hard physical labor, which breaks down their bodies faster than those that require use of a person's mind to accomplish their tasks. People who use their bodies to earn a living are not only paid less, they are out of the labor market 15 years sooner than those who use their minds to earn a living.

> *Myth:* **A major cause of poverty is alcoholism and drug addiction.**

Fact: People in poverty are no more likely than their wealthier counterparts to struggle with the disease of alcoholism or other addictions. Although drug sales may be more visible in low-income neighborhoods, drug use and addictions happen in all social classes. Studies have found that alcohol consumption is significantly higher among upper-middle-class white high school students than among poor black high school students. This finding supports a history of research showing that alcohol abuse is far more prevalent among wealthy people than among people who live in poverty. Recently, the Centers for Disease Control has reported that "the rich out-drink the poor by 27.4 percent." Their report shows that 45.2 percent of adults from households whose incomes are below the poverty line report having consumed at least one alcoholic beverage in the past 30 days, compared with 72.6 percent of adults whose household incomes are at least four times the poverty level.

> *Myth:* **Welfare moms are getting rich by having babies!**

Fact: Women in poverty don't have children because of money, but because having children in their lives is so important to them. To them, the meaning of having children is to love them and have someone who will love them back. They often have many role models who have shown them how to be a mom and have helped create a strong desire to be a mom (often feeling it was the reason they were born, the main purpose in their life). Since they have not been exposed to a middle-class lifestyle, they have not been exposed to middle-class concerns (such as: Do we have enough money to pay for their college tuition? Do we live in the right neighborhood so they will be able to attend the good schools? Do we have health insurance to help cover all their medical needs? Do we have the right type of car and car seat so we will be able to keep them safe?). Expectations are set by what you experience as a child. If you have never gone to a "good school," lived in the "right neighborhood," or had preventive health care, how would you know that you needed it? Having a child is a natural human desire. People all over the world have babies without having money for college tuition. Just because you are in poverty does not mean that you do not want to fulfill these natural human desires. People in poverty are people with the same emotions and desires as people who are not in poverty. The reality is that some of us live in a context where we learn about the value of education or gaining a skill, while others have not had that luxury.

Some believe that the reason women in poverty have babies is to obtain welfare. The facts show that welfare is not a significant incentive for having children. In 23 states, when a new baby is born to a family already on welfare, they receive no additional cash per month. In the remaining states, welfare recipients receive an average of $60 per month to care for a baby—which is well below the cost of raising a child. In addition, the average welfare family is no larger than the average non-recipient American family—with welfare families having 1.9 children and non-welfare families averaging 1.86.

Myth: We've made welfare too easy and too comfortable. If we stopped coddling them, they wouldn't stay in the system.

Fact: In 1986, a welfare check for a family of three was $408 per month and they received $150 in food stamps. Rent was approximately $395—leaving $13 per month to pay for utilities, insurance, sundries, etc. In 2016, a welfare check for a family of three was $478 per month—a $70 per month increase. Rent is now $750—almost double. Of those who receive welfare assistance, more than half stop receiving benefits after a year, 70 percent within two years, and 85 percent within four years.

> **Myth:** There is too much obesity in America—especially among the poor—to believe that we really have issues with hunger and food insecurity.

Fact: For years, low-income individuals received food stamps to assist with their families' needs. Today, the Supplemental Nutrition Assistance Program (SNAP) offers nutrition assistance to millions of eligible low-income individuals and families and provides economic benefits to communities. Below are a couple of examples of what families can expect to receive on a monthly basis:

	Gross Amount	Per Person	Per Meal
Family of 3	$511	$170.33	$1.89
Family of 4	$649	$162.25	$1.80

As of January 2016, 45.4 million persons were participating in SNAP. In total, 76 percent of SNAP benefits go toward households with children, 11.9 percent go to households with disabled persons, and 10 percent go to households with senior citizens.

In addition, food that is nutritious is very expensive. The food that can be bought on a budget, as outlined above, is full of carbohydrates and refined sugar. Also, people in poverty often have to pay more for the same items their wealthier counterparts get for a better price. People with more resources can buy in bulk, thus saving more money per item. People in poverty often have to shop at their neighborhood convenience store, where the items cost more than they do in grocery stores.

> **Myth:** They can't be that poor when they can afford to buy big-screen TVs and new cell phones; pay for services such as manicures/pedicures, tattoos, and piercings; or when they spend a lot of their money on cigarettes and booze or to gamble.

Fact: Paulo Freire, in his book *Pedagogy of the Oppressed*, says every society teaches its members what it takes to belong. People in poverty feel that no one notices them—no one looks up at them when they enter a room, no one makes eye contact, no one talks to them. But when they have an item that is highly valued in American society (like a big-screen TV or a new cell phone), they receive societal honor—an automatic respect that provides a temporary way to feel like "somebody," like they belong. For just a second, they may get noticed. They feel like "they are somebody." The same is true for manicures/pedicures, tattoos, and piercing. If we do something that adorns our body and makes us feel pretty or gets us noticed, our value goes up. Again, we feel like we are somebody!

Needing to feel like you belong, that you are somebody, is not unique to those living in poverty. It is a human need that Maslow puts right up there with the human need to eat. We will do anything to belong. In fact, studies have shown that the people with the most debt in the United States are those in the middle class. They know the value (intrinsically and extrinsically) of having the right house; living in the right neighborhood; driving the right car; and wearing the right clothes, shoes, and jewelry.

Attitudes and Beliefs

Before we can relate to and communicate more effectively with people living in poverty, we must make an effort to examine our personal beliefs and open our minds to new interpretations of the behavior of those struggling to meet their basic needs. Attitudes and beliefs shape tone of voice, body posture, facial expressions, and actions toward others. Our judgments impede connection and understanding. Therefore, we need to reflect on our perception and understanding of poverty and the people who live in it.

Perception

Perception is how our mind makes sense of the world. It is shaped by our upbringing and the adults we grow up with. Because the media are the number-one teachers of poverty, perceptions about poverty and the people who live in it are often based on stereotypes and myths. Can you imagine going to a new country and trying to teach or work in a service profession without any previous knowledge of the daily lives of the people who live there?

To understand and relate, we must examine our own attitudes, beliefs, and perceptions about poverty and the people who live in it. Gaining knowledge of poverty causes and impacts assists us in meeting people where they are. It helps us to suspend judgment and better understand behavior, priorities, and experiences. Being poverty informed changes our judgment and perceptions and allows us to communicate and relate in empowering ways.

CASE STUDY

Think back to or reread the case study at the beginning of this guidebook, and then carefully read and reflect on the following questions:

From your perception, which facts on poverty might be contributing to the barriers for this family?

When reading the case study, did you find yourself thinking about any of the myths and stereotypes about poverty (pages 10-12)? If yes, how can you turn those thoughts around?

In the video, Dr. Beegle talked about her feelings while growing up that "people don't care." What can you do to show Jeffrey and Colleen that you really care?

You have 10 years of a life story built into this case study. When someone comes to you for assistance, how much do you know about that person and their situation? What more do you need to know about this family so you have a better understanding of their situation? How might you learn this information?

Segment 2: Insider's Perspective

> **Guiding Questions**
> - What was it like to be born into the deepest poverty in America?
> - What can we learn from an insider perspective?
> - What efforts made the most difference?
> - Practical tips from lessons learned

Why an Insider's Perspective?

The majority of research and writing about poverty are done by people who have not experienced poverty. In this segment, Dr. Donna M. Beegle shares an insider's perspective on what it is like to survive without a home, education, or skills to earn a living wage in a country that is known for its wealth and opportunities. She shares generational poverty experiences that deeply impacted her learning and potential.

While her generational poverty experiences are not representative of all poverty experiences, her research and work have shown that the practices used to break barriers for people in generational poverty can also be effective for people from working-class, immigrant, and situational poverty. On the contrary, strategies used to break poverty barriers based on race and/or situational poverty only often fall short of addressing generational and working-class poverty barriers.

Dr. Beegle uses her personal story of being born into generational poverty—along with nearly three decades of research on what works—to illuminate the perspectives of people who live in generational, working-class, immigrant, situational, and mixed-class poverty. To effectively fight poverty, we must understand the many different life experiences of poverty and how each impacts our Neighbors' abilities to move forward.

Excerpt from the Donna M. Beegle Story

I was born into a large, loving family! But, at an early age, I also learned that I had been born into a community where everyone was in crisis. I was born into the deepest poverty in America—generational poverty. In the war zone of poverty, I soon felt the sting of the poverty "bullets" of hunger, untreated health issues, limited or inadequate access to transportation, constant evictions, being made fun of and not wanted, and never enough money to make ends meet. I learned how these "bullets" would constantly knock us down and wound us physically, mentally, and emotionally.

Generational poverty means that you cannot hide the impacts of poverty. Every family member—including the children—is present for the evictions and hunger. Most families in generational poverty like mine live a lifetime with poor nutrition. If we were in school long enough and could figure out the paperwork, we got signed up for free lunch. But, we often declined the free lunch to prevent the shame and stigma that were served with the free meal. Many nights our dinner was just a spoonful of peanut butter or government cheese melted over tortilla chips. We rarely, if ever, had fresh vegetables or fruit.

Our families suffer because there is no health insurance or money for dental care. It is a world where the emergency room is your doctor, not a "family physician" who knows you well. There are no annual checkups or preventive care to ensure health.

Generational poverty also means that, for many generations, most of my family members were illiterate—with many of them making an "x" for their names when signing paperwork. Because of our limited literacy, inadequate/incomplete education, and lack of specific job skills, we could not get a job that would earn a living wage. My family members subsisted on temporary and seasonal work, migrant labor, and minimum-wage jobs—often requiring hard physical labor. While I was growing up, our family's biggest focus was making it through the day.

As with other families from generational poverty, my immediate family was highly mobile. We lived in multiple residences over my lifetime, including condemned rental houses, roach- and rat-infested motel rooms, trailers, storage units, and campgrounds. I can't remember a time when there weren't multiple generations and multiple extended family members living together under one small roof. Whenever necessary and possible, we slept in our cars or at relatives' homes. Sometimes, the river was our bath, while the gas station was our restroom.

My early experiences in impoverished schools shaped my views about myself and my expectations for the future—much like they did for my brothers. In school, I didn't understand what was going on. I didn't know the words my teachers used—as I was unable to understand and speak in their middle-class language. Every other sentence I spoke contained the word "ain't." I didn't know when it was proper to say "gone" or "went," "seen" or "saw." I didn't know the middle-class examples teachers used to explain the academic subjects. This just reinforced that there was something wrong with me and my family and friends. It reinforced that education was not for me or people like me. I internalized the poverty and its associated deficiencies to such a degree that I did not believe I was smart or had anything to offer. I lost all hope and, like many people in generational poverty, I lived in survival mode.

Sex roles tend to be more rigid in poverty. Like most males in poverty, the men in my family were socialized that they were "the protectors and providers" for their families. But, because they were born into poverty, they were not able to fulfill their societal role through obtaining a living-wage job. By around the age of 10, they started seeing the poverty and believing they needed to make it okay for the women in their lives. Sometimes, because their families are experiencing poverty, men are often forced to leave their families in order for them to obtain services and get assistance. All my brothers did extraordinary things—all dropped out of school before graduating, one left the family, and others worked long, hard hours in unsafe jobs—to help the family survive.

My brothers also had to go outside the law—including sacrificing their reputations and giving up their freedom—to help the family survive. I can say I am the only member of my family who has not been incarcerated—not because I have never broken the law, but because I have been well protected by my loving brothers and allowed to follow more female roles. My brothers have been jailed for minor offenses such as failure to pay child support, failure to pay fines for driving without car insurance, outstanding tickets, writing bad checks, and digging in dumpsters for cardboard/bottles for recycling. Others were put in for longer periods of time for offenses such as burglary—stealing things to make life easier for the family or to sell the items they stole to get money to pay the bills. I do not condone stealing. But, because of growing up in poverty, I learned to understand how and why it happens. My brothers were not genetically programmed to take the things our family needed or to break the law, but surviving in the war zone of poverty often requires those skills.

At 15 years old—after all the shame and humiliation at school, I dropped out to get married. When we married, Jerry was 18 years old and had only a seventh-grade education from impoverished schools. He could read and write at about a second-grade level. We had our honeymoon in a cherry field in Wenatchee, Washington—meaning that after the wedding ceremony we drove to Wenatchee and went straight to work picking cherries. Jerry and I soon began working full time for minimum wage at a foam rubber factory in Portland, Oregon. I had to lie about my age since it was illegal to hire a 15-year-old. Here, our adult life became a repeat of our childhoods. We worked hard but still had to make choices between rent and utilities. We continued to struggle with hunger, evictions, and not having our fundamental human needs met.

My dream—for as long as I could remember—was to be a mom. So, I got pregnant right after turning 17. During my pregnancy, I rarely saw a doctor and was not eligible for a medical card because Jerry was in the home and earning minimum wage at the foam rubber factory. My mom was my "doctor" and her education was from having six kids of her own. By the time I finally saw a doctor, he told me the baby was barely hanging in there. Joyce Marie was born almost three months early. She weighed one pound, nine ounces, and was eight and a half inches long. She only lived for nine hours since her lungs were just too tiny to survive. I was devastated by her death.

My solution to the heartbreak of losing my daughter Joyce (and to fulfill my dream of being a mom) was to get pregnant as soon as possible. As with my first pregnancy, prenatal care and healthy foods were not part of my life. I was so afraid this baby would die just like Joyce Marie, but welfare policy would still not allow me to receive a medical card if Jerry was in the home. So, when I got afraid I would lose this baby too, I lied to the welfare worker and said Jerry had left me. Because of that lie, I got a medical card in my fourth month of pregnancy. On March 23, 1979, Jennifer Marie was born two months prematurely. She was immediately put on a respirator and had an IV inserted into her stomach. When she was 11 days old, she underwent emergency heart surgery to close a hole in her heart. She had a 50 percent chance of surviving the surgery, and, if she lived, she would likely suffer from blindness and/or mental challenges. Jennifer survived the heart surgery and was kept on a respirator for two months. After two and a half months, when she finally weighed five pounds, I was able to take her home.

Since Jennifer was considered high risk, Oregon Health Sciences University staff recommended that she receive priority placement for Head Start (HS), our nation's preschool program for children in poverty. The HS staff linked our family to the resources we desperately needed (e.g., the Women, Infants, and Children [WIC] nutrition program, which provides juice, milk, and healthy foods to moms and their young children; temporary housing so we could move out of the car in which we were living, etc.). I am convinced that it is due to these resources that I got to leave the hospital for the first time after three pregnancies with a healthy baby boy. Daniel weighed six pounds and six ounces.

During our marriage, Jerry and I subsisted on low-wage jobs—working in migrant labor, pizza parlors, retail, and manufacturing—or welfare. We moved from place to place, hoping for a better life. But we still could not earn enough to meet our basic needs. Just like we had experienced growing up, we continued to have no health care. Our food was limited and our nutritional needs were not being met. The stress of poverty finally took a toll on our marriage. Jerry and I divorced after 10 years. By the age of 25, I was alone trying to care for my six-year-old daughter (who was in the first grade) and two-year-old son. It wasn't long before we, too, were again evicted and homeless.

As a single mom, I applied for welfare. We were given $408 plus $150 in food stamps per month. With this, I found a place I could rent for $395 a month. Our house, located in a high-poverty/high-crime community, was broken into five times in a four-month period. With the remaining $13 after paying rent, I had to pay for utilities and transportation; buy clothing, soap, shampoo, toilet paper, and other basic necessities; and go to the Laundromat. I was constantly making impossible choices—pay the rent or pay the bills; have my utilities shut off or get evicted.

After several months of juggling my payments like this, we were given an eviction notice and our lights were turned off for nonpayment. I went to a Community Action Agency to ask for help. The caseworker told me there was a new pilot welfare-to-work program, called Women in Transition (WIT), that was designed to be a three-week life skills program for displaced homemakers. Its goal was to help single women gain an education or skills to earn a living for their families.

At that point in my life, I had no hope or belief that a program could help me. I went to check it out—not thinking it would change anything, but not knowing what else to do. After the program director talked about the WIT program components, she informed us that we would be eligible for a Section 8 housing certificate if we completed the three-week program. No one in my family—although we lived for several generations with no place to call home—had qualified for housing assistance, since we never had the right address or right identification, or even knew how to fill out the paperwork for accessing housing support. Then and there I made up my mind—I would complete the program and secure housing so my babies would not be on the streets!

I went into the program just to get housing, but the four middle-class women who were running the pilot program took the time to get to know me. They made phone calls on my behalf and navigated me to resources and opportunities. They showed me that I was not stupid—that the things I was doing in my everyday life to survive were skills often used in professional job descriptions. I began to feel "taller." They were teaching me that poverty was the problem, not me or my family. They believed in me when I did not believe in myself. They were relentless and persistent and did not give up on me. When life knocked me down, they were there to connect me to a resource or opportunity to overcome it.

The women in the WIT program shared their stories of living in a middle-class world. I had never heard stories before that illustrated a middle-class life. I had believed that everyone was born to migrant labor parents, and only knew their stories. The program staff helped me realize that they were just people who had different life experiences (such as living in only one house and going to only one school while they were young, being born to educated parents, never worrying about food or having their basic needs met). They taught me to dream. They taught me how to take what I knew and explore careers that would build upon this knowledge.

I completed the WIT program believing that I had something to offer. At last, I had a glimmer of hope. I wrote my dream in my diary: "I want to get a GED (general equivalency diploma) and maybe someday take a journalism class. Then, I will be somebody and be able to take care of Jennifer and Daniel." This passionate motivation to take care of my two children remained constant throughout my educational journey. Supported by the four women from the WIT program and with government resources to meet my family's basic needs, I was able to reach a milestone and attain my GED at the age of 26.

Armed with hope, newfound confidence, and my WIT action plan, I went to my welfare worker and told her I wanted to pursue a two-year degree in journalism so I would not need government assistance anymore. She quickly told me that the state and federal welfare policies dictate that, in order to qualify for welfare, I needed to be available for any minimum-wage job. If I were in school, I wouldn't be available, so the government would sanction me and cut my welfare check from $408 to $258 a month. After much thought, I told the welfare worker, "Go ahead and cut my check if that's what you have to do. But I'm not going back to poverty. I'm going to college!"

At this time, the primary supports that kept me moving forward in the educational system were the housing voucher that assisted me in having my housing needs met; the continued support of my family; and having mentors from the WIT program and Mt. Hood Community College/ University of Portland who believed in me, encouraged me, and helped me navigate resources and opportunities while I journeyed the unknown path to higher education. Within 10 years, I earned an A.A. in journalism, a B.A. in communications, an M.A. in communication with a minor in gender studies, and an Ed.D. in educational leadership.

Today, I share my life experiences along with the insights I gained from years of studying poverty as I speak to and train educators, justice professionals, health care providers, social service providers, and other professionals across the nation who want to make a difference for those living in the crisis of poverty. For the past 26 years, I have traveled to hundreds of cities, covering 50 states and five countries to assist professionals with proven strategies for breaking poverty barriers.

What Efforts Made the Most Difference? Strategies to Break Poverty Barriers

Below are five research-based theories on helping people move out of poverty, along with some of the ways these were evidenced in Dr. Beegle's story.

Theory	Personal Perspective
1. **Strengths Perspective Approach**: Every individual has strengths and potential. You can empower people by focusing on what is good about them, what they do know, what skills they already have, and what their dreams are.	The staff in the Women in Transition (WIT) program helped rebuild Donna's self-confidence and hope by helping her see what was good about her and helping her discover her knowledge and skills. They had her list what she did in a day, then matched those duties to careers on a professional job skills list (and showed her how much money she could make by doing those things for a living!). For instance, "You take good care of your kids. You could be a daycare worker." "You have been managing your money when you have it. You could be an accountant."
2. **Resiliency**: The ability to cope and continue functioning, despite experiencing stress and adversity. It is not a personal trait. Resiliency comes from the environment and how people are treated. Treat people special and illuminate talents/skills that can be used to earn a living.	Donna was born the fifth of six children. Because she was the only girl, she was treated as special and different by her parents, brothers, and other relatives. Donna was in the pilot program Women in Transition. Her group got housing and extensive mentoring. There was no housing for group two, and elected officials decided that the hope and confidence rebuilding activities were too "touchy feely"—so they were removed from the program.
3. **Asset Theory**: The more assets a person has, both internal (hope, confidence, conflict resolution skills, sense of purpose, etc.) and external (mentors, housing, transportation, etc.), the more likely they will break out of the iron cage of poverty.	In Donna's story, you hear how she had both external and internal assets. Her internal assets included her belief that she was special and that her family loved and cared for her. Her external assets included a resourceful mom who taught her that "no" means "ask someone else." She is the first to obtain subsidized housing, which provided the stability for her to work on her GED. Four women from the middle class took the time to mentor her and navigate resources she needed to break barriers. Her mom and cousin Lynda watched her kids while she completed her education. Her brother Wayne helped her with her homework. Her other brothers helped keep her car running and repaired her heater.

Theory	Personal Perspective
4. **Social Capital Theory**: No one succeeds alone. Those who are successful have connections with others who support them in various ways. People in poverty need the same kinds of supports; they need meaningful relationships with others who are educated and skilled and know how to navigate the middle-class world. The isolation of poverty perpetuates it. People in poverty need as many people in their address book who are not fighting poverty as they have who are. Those not in poverty can expose people to possibilities and assist in navigating resources and opportunities for moving out of poverty.	The staff from the WIT program realized that no one was successful alone. Although the program was designed to be only three weeks long, they vowed to help Donna for as long as it took and do whatever was needed. They helped her learn middle-class language and helped her navigate the education system. They also took her to places and introduced her to people who could help her in her journey (such as, they took her to Mt. Hood Community College and introduced her to a financial aid person and to the jobs person—including telling her how they were like her so she could build identification and see how she was like them).
5. **Faulty Attribution Theory**: When we attribute motives to someone else's behavior without discovering the "why" behind their actions.	Donna stated how she had a smart mouth and attitude because of the impacts of poverty on her life. She told a story of the Community Action Agency staff person who first told her about the WIT program. When the woman told her about the program, Donna sarcastically said, "Why don't you go do the program?" Luckily for Donna, the woman understood why Donna acted that way and did not take it personally. She just moved past it. She knew that it had nothing to do with her, but rather it had everything to do with Donna's lifetime in poverty.

Below are practical strategies (navigating/mentoring practices) for each theory that you can start using right away.

Strengths Perspective Approach:

- Stand in awe of those fighting poverty.
- Believe in the unlimited potential of every person you meet. We cannot know what they might do, but we can limit possibilities with low expectations.
- Look for strengths and skills that can be built upon and provide opportunities to earn a living.
- State directly what you believe is good about them.
- Find ways for people to shine. Learn about their skills and ask them to help you. Build a relationship where they are included and needed.
- Tell people you are happy to see them (even when they are late or have not met a deadline). Give the benefit of the doubt that there is a reason for their behavior or actions that makes sense from their perspective.
- Practice showing empathy instead of sympathy (no one wants pity or judgment). Empathy is understanding from their perspective how they feel and what they are experiencing. Sympathy is feeling sorry for and staying distant from the person/situation.

Resiliency:
- Treat people special.
- Illuminate how they are different from most people. Show them what is unique about them.
- Notice and state when you see a skill, talent, or demonstration of knowledge and compliment overtly.
- Practice a "strengths-based approach" when communicating with people in poverty using the strategies listed above to increase a person's resiliency.

Asset Theory:
- Listen carefully to a person's narrative. In their stories, you can learn how they feel, what is in their way, and what they care about.
- Learn what assets a person has and what services or opportunities are needed; connect them to people who can assist with removing obstacles and building their capacities to succeed.
- Build partnerships in your community so that you know where to find resources.
- Help people navigate the middle-class world. Make phone calls; offer to work with them to fill out necessary paperwork; explain complex information in simple terms.
- Teach people how to advocate for themselves. Tell them what questions to ask, role-play what they are going to experience and how they can be most successful, explain how systems work, suggest programs or services you know will help.
- Visit the Search Institute for 40 developmental assets that enhance success. (To download, go to www.search-institute.org/developmental-assets.) Review these assets and determine ways to develop these assets with those you are working to empower.

Social Capital Theory:
- Introduce people to others who have benefited from education or a living-wage job.
- Tell people about opportunities (programs, events, etc.) that you know will put them in a place to build relationships with people who are educated.
- Make connections face-to-face, instead of giving phone numbers or a "list" of people/agencies to call.
- Help people obtain tools, resources, and knowledge they need to feel like they "belong" in the environment and with the people you are connecting them with (clothes, materials, knowledge of etiquette, etc.).
- Find out their interests and introduce them to successful people who are doing those jobs or careers.
- Give people address books and your contact information.

Faulty Attribution Theory:

- Seek to understand the "why" behind behavior from the perspective of the person you are working to empower.
- Withhold judgment. Recognize that from their perspective, with the resources and knowledge they have, the behavior made sense at that time. That does not mean you have to agree, but seek to understand and show other ways of handling situations.
- Tell yourself people are doing the best they can with the information and perspectives they currently possess.
- Remind yourself that your experiences and worldview may be different from those of the people you serve.
- Pay attention when you catch yourself attributing motive (they are lazy, not motivated, etc.) to someone's behavior. We are not powerful enough to know the "why" behind others' actions. More often, we are attributing motive based on what we would have done in that situation and not understanding they have not had our resources, experiences, and exposures.

Practical Tips

- Listen first. Use phrases like, "Help me understand." It helps to know from their perspective what is most important, what they want to happen, and their dreams.
- Pull out strengths from their stories and brag on them. Tell them how that strength can be used to earn a living.
- Find out what's in their way of moving out of poverty. Focus on what they perceive is stopping them from doing what they want to do. Listening helps you separate the people from the poverty—you learn about their strengths, interests, what they want to do/need, and what motivates them.
- Build common ground by telling your story or sharing how you are like the person.
- Find a hundred ways to tell people what is right about them. Help them shine! Give them a compliment.
- Identify "belonging behaviors" and help people feel like they belong and are accepted.
- Develop a comprehensive approach. Build your backpack of resources.
- Examine policies/rules and ensure they are meeting people where they are, not where we want them to be.

CASE STUDY

Reflecting on the case study, review and answer the following questions:

- Make a list of the strengths you see in Jeffrey. What talents does Colleen have? What are their strengths as a family?

- Write down comments you could say directly to each of them that would highlight their strengths.

- Make a list of what you have in common with Jeffrey and Colleen. Write down comments you could say to build common ground.

- List three ways that you can help them feel like you want to work with them during your first meeting.

- In what ways can you help Jeffrey and Colleen with their current situation?

- Whom else do you need to involve to remove barriers and assist them in accessing resources and opportunities to move out of poverty?

- If there are areas they need assistance with that are not part of your knowledge or skill set, whom do you have in your resource backpack that you can connect them with?

- Are there policies or rules that might get in your way of empowering Jeffrey or Colleen? Are there things that might be changed to serve them better?

Segment 3: What Does the Word Poverty Mean?

Guiding Questions

- What is the definition of "poverty"?
- What are some of the different types of poverty?
- How do each of these lived experiences of poverty impact our Neighbors?

"Poverty: The state of one who lacks a usual or socially acceptable amount of money or material possessions."
—Merriam-Webster Dictionary

The word poverty is used to describe many different lived experiences. Without a clear understanding of the diverse kinds of poverty in America, there is a tendency to treat all people as if they live in the same conditions and to create policies and strategies that may only impact a certain population of people who are living in poverty. Most services in America are set up to serve people facing situational poverty. These are people who grow up in a middle-class context but fall into poverty because of a health issue, job loss, divorce, etc. For this group, a little bit of help can usually get them back on their feet. However, for other types of poverty, a little bit of help just assists them in coping and does not provide the necessary resources and opportunities needed to move out and stay out of poverty.

In this segment, we will review the federal definition of poverty and learn how the formula to calculate what a family needs today is still based on a 1960s cost of living. We will examine the differences impacting people's lived experiences in the 21st century. In addition, we will explore four of the many different poverty experiences.

Federal Poverty Guidelines

The current federal poverty guideline for a family of four is $24,300. This is what the federal government says a family of four needs to meet their needs. If you think it seems low, it is. The number we currently use to determine who gets help is based on a 1960s cost-of-living formula. In a 1955 government study, it was reported that Americans spent approximately one-third of their after-tax income on food. A bureaucrat in the Social Security Administration took the Department of Agriculture's lowest food plan for an American family—one designed for temporary or emergency use when funds were low—and multiplied by a factor of three to create the federal poverty guideline (Hammond, 2005).

Today, the largest expenditure in a family budget is housing. The 1960 designation has not changed to reflect this expenditure, nor does it account for the changes in family dynamics and basic survival needs that have occurred since the 1960s. For example, more women are in the workplace now, creating a need for child care. Child care expense is not calculated into the 1960s formula because economists in the '60s believed there would be a parent in the home. They also did not include transportation as a family expense. They presumed that people would walk to work. Both of these huge family expenses are ignored by the current use of this formula. In addition, health insurance is also not included as a family expense. Economists projected that employers would cover health insurance.

The Economic Policy Institute added in health care, child care, and transportation costs and found a family of four would need $48,000 to meet their basic needs. Not only does the federal poverty guideline fall short for people who make under $24,300, but it does not offer any help to families with incomes between $24,250 and $48,000. These families are not meeting their basic needs and they don't qualify for most government services such as welfare, food stamps, rent assistance, Head Start, or Pell Grants.

Contexts of Poverty

Scholar Lisbeth Schorr studied what it takes to assist people to move out of poverty. In her book *Within Our Reach*, she states that one of the core criteria for breaking poverty barriers is to meet people where they are, not where we want them to be. Familiarity with the various lived experiences called poverty provides a foundation for developing solutions that meet people where they are. What people know is based on their lived experiences. Each of their life experiences shapes expectations, knowledge, confidence, and opportunities for gaining a skill or an education.

The word "poverty" is used to describe many different life situations. Below are some experiences people may face in the different types of poverty. For each, there are common circumstances and environmental factors that shape the worldview, behavior, and norms of the individuals who experience them. These are intended to provide a general idea of what each context is like. Of course, there are always exceptions, because people are complex. Understanding the typical experiences people are having in each context prepares us to actively listen to a person's experiences and tailor our efforts so we can meet people where they are.

Generational Poverty

- This is the deepest poverty. People experiencing this type of poverty are born into a world where multiple barriers exist.
- Society teaches them that "we all start the same and have the same opportunities," so they start to believe "there must be something wrong with me and my family."
- They get strong societal messages that "if you work hard, you will succeed."
- They are workers of the land, as opposed to owners of the land.
- Housing is unstable or nonexistent.
- Family members work in temporary, part-time, unskilled, low-paying jobs or subsist on disability or subsistence welfare.
- They are isolated from people who are educated or earn a living wage.
- Families are highly mobile, moving frequently to look for work.
- There is low family literacy; children move from high-poverty schools to other high-poverty schools that are not equipped to address the impacts of poverty.
- No matter what they do, life seems to throw more obstacles in their way and knock them down.
- Their focus is on making it through the day.
- They have strong family loyalty.
- They have a strong willingness to give to and help one another.
- Their world of survival creates skill sets for making something out of nothing.
- They feel hopeless.
- Poverty is viewed as a personal deficiency.

Life Outlook: *Life happens to me. I don't have any control over it.*

Working-Class Poverty

- This type of poverty teaches that "if you work hard, you will succeed."
- They receive strong messages that "the individual is the reason for continued poverty."
- They are working but barely able to pay for basic needs (no money for any extras).
- They live paycheck to paycheck.
- They may use a different sentence structure than educated, middle-class people.
- Few have health care.

- They are renters as opposed to homeowners.
- Their focus is on making it two weeks or through the month.
- Their self-confidence and self-esteem are impacted by an inability to "move up" in the workplace due to lack of education and skills.
- They feel hopeless.
- Their poverty is seen as a personal deficiency.

> **Life Outlook**: *"I have some control over my life, but not very much."*

Immigrant Poverty

- This type of poverty includes the struggles with food, shelter, and basic needs; plus, it also has additional barriers.
- They receive strong societal messages that there are societal causes for the poverty (such as a broken economic system, lack of infrastructure, etc.).
- Many come to the U.S. with little or no external resources.
- They face language and cultural barriers.
- They experience racism and isolation.
- They have stronger self-esteem and self-confidence than those experiencing poverty who were born in the U.S.
- They have hope.
- They often do better in school and the workplace than those born into poverty in America.
- Their poverty is viewed as a system problem.

> **Life Outlook:** *"I have the power to make a better life for me and my family."*

Situational Poverty

- This type of poverty teaches that there is a reason for the poverty (divorce, job loss, etc.).
- They grow up in a stable environment with their basic needs met—and more.
- They attended school regularly.
- They communicate in middle-class style, words, and sentence structure.
- They understand middle-class norms.

- They know what it takes to be successful.
- They have been surrounded by educated people with living-wage jobs and lots of possibilities.
- As adults, they experience a crisis (e.g., health issue, downsizing) and their income drops.
- They are often able to make it back to the middle class.
- They may become isolated from middle-class friends.
- They do not know how to use poverty resources (welfare, food stamps, etc.).
- They experience shame and embarrassment but understand the reason for their poverty.
- They have not internalized their poverty as a personal deficiency.
- They may not recognize the advantages of growing up middle class; they can become harsh judges of others experiencing generational or working-class poverty.

Life Outlook: *"I pulled myself out of poverty. If I did it, anyone can— you just have to make better choices, work harder, and make sacrifices."*

These are just four of many lived experiences of poverty. There are also mixed-class poverty experiences. An example of this would include being born to a parent from situational poverty and a parent who experienced working-class poverty. A child in this context will receive different messages than a child born to two parents from generational poverty.

The goal of learning about the many types of poverty is not to "identify" what type your Neighbor is experiencing, but rather to open your mind and not assume that people have capacities, exposure, and experiences that they may not have had. Becoming informed about the many lived experiences of poverty provides a foundation for understanding your Neighbor's worldview, expectations, motivations, and communication.

The term poverty is used to describe many lived experiences, not a monolithic one. This knowledge will empower you to listen better to your Neighbors and to not make assumptions about their experiences. It will also provide you with the tools and strategies for better serving those living in the crisis of poverty. This insight provides the foundation for working with your Neighbor to address the obstacles they see as preventing them from moving forward.

Poverty Crosses Race

Poverty is often perceived as a racial or ethnic issue. Some minorities are indeed overrepresented among those in poverty, but not all. Compared with an overall poverty rate of 13.5 percent, for example, 24.1 percent of Blacks were categorized as living in poverty in 2016, and 21.4 percent in that same category were Hispanic. For Asians, however, the figure was 11.4 percent. This compares with a poverty rate of 9.1 percent for Whites (U.S. Census, 2016). It is important to note that the majority (in total numbers—over 41 percent) of people in poverty in 2015 in the United States were White, with a total number of almost 18 million (U.S. Census, 2016)

Number in Poverty and Poverty Rates by Race/Ethnicity (2014)		
Race/Ethnicity	Number (in Millions)	Poverty Rate
All Races	43.1	13.5%
White	17.8	9.1%
Black	10	24.1%
Hispanic (Of Any Race)	12.1	21.4%
Asian	2.1	11.4%

Source: U.S. Census Data collected in 2015/ reported in 2016.

Research studies on poverty often focus on those groups with the highest percentages in poverty (i.e., African Americans or Latinos), while giving less thought and consideration to the group with the largest number of people in poverty (Whites). Educational and public service professionals and organizations often frame their services to provide extra assistance to minorities. But, poverty needs to be acknowledged as a large-scale societal problem that cuts across racial/ethnic lines. Special attention should be paid to the voices and needs of all those in poverty who have often been marginalized, ignored, and treated as invisible.

The bullets of poverty hit all races and ethnicities equally. If you are homeless, hungry, hurting—no matter your race or ethnicity—these all feel the same and impact the people in the same way. Thus, when creating policies and procedures, individuals and organizations need to make sure they are looking at the impacts of poverty across race and ethnicity. In addition to the poverty issues, race and ethnicity compound the impacts of poverty. These individuals must also deal with the additional bullets of racism, language, and cultural barriers. Efforts to combat racism need to be equally strong as those to combat the poverty. If a person is in poverty and facing racism, language, and cultural barriers, she or he has three major barriers to reaching their fullest potential.

CASE STUDY

Reflecting on the case study, review and answer the following questions:

- From what you have learned in this segment, what lived experience(s) of poverty have Jeffrey and Colleen lived?

- Write down what life has taught Jeffrey and Colleen about working.

- Make a list of what it might take for the family to earn a living wage.

- Write down skills or knowledge you could share to leave this family in a better place.

- Identify skills or resources that could help the family that you do not have and list who in your organization or community might provide those supports. Practice Dr. Beegle's mantra: "If not me, then who?"

- If Jeffrey and Colleen were African American, what additional considerations would you need to keep in mind when working to empower them to move out of poverty?

- If Jeffrey and Colleen were Hispanic and did not speak English, what additional considerations would you need to keep in mind when serving them?

Segment 4: Understanding the Perspectives of People in Poverty

> **Guiding Questions**
> - What is it like for our Neighbors to interact with volunteers and helping professionals?
> - How can we build common ground with our Neighbors in poverty?

We have often heard it said that "poverty is just a mindset or choice." Well, wouldn't it be nice if a person could just change their mind and they would no longer be homeless or hungry? Unfortunately, poverty is not a mindset. People can change their minds and make different choices all day long, but without skills, education, and access to opportunities, they will still struggle to earn a living. Poverty steals hope and self-confidence, which gets in the way of moving out and staying out of poverty!

Social Class Context Shapes Worldview

We learn about our world and develop attitudes, beliefs, and values from our daily life experiences. If your family struggles with hunger, your daily life experiences will be shaped by that. If your family owns their home, your daily life experiences will be impacted by that. If you watch people you love do without their basic needs, you will be affected by that. Every adult who comes into the life of a child is handing that child a description of the world. People can only teach and model what they have been exposed to in a relevant and meaningful way. Examples include:

- The ways that you bathe, eat, dress, talk, and laugh are all taught by the people you have meaningful relationships with.
- The way that you believe others should behave is based on your expectations from your own learned norms.
- The ways that you celebrate holidays and special events (such as birthdays)—and how you act during family gatherings—all relate to your experiences in your context. You learned through communication from those around you how to "be" and what to "expect" on those days.

The Worldview Taught by Poverty

People living in poverty internalize the messages sent their way by society. Families living in the crisis of poverty receive societal messages that they do not belong and that they are the cause of their own poverty. Many people come to believe that something is wrong with them. Poverty steals their hope and self-confidence. Here are some of the messages taught to people of all ages experiencing generational and working-class poverty:

- People who are making it do not care about me.
- Everyone else seems smarter than I am.
- People who are not in poverty are somehow better than I am.
- I/we don't belong.
- People like us don't get educated.
- The purpose of education is unclear.
- We don't have what we need to break out of poverty.
- There is no one to help us.

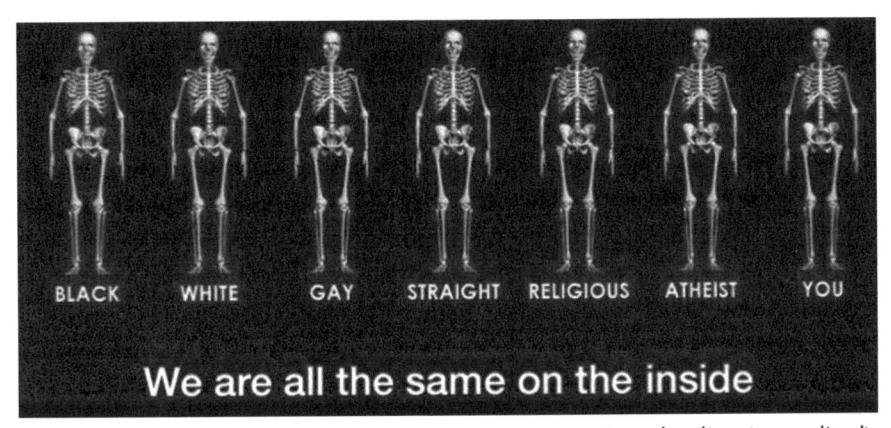

BLACK   WHITE   GAY   STRAIGHT   RELIGIOUS   ATHEIST   YOU

We are all the same on the inside

Found online (uncredited).

As the meme above is trying to show, when we get down to the bare bones, we are more alike than different. We are all part of the human race with similar feelings and emotions. There are certain things that we all need to survive—such as nutritious food, water, health care, a safe place to live. We are the same species, but our life experiences affect what access we have to developing our potentials. Life experiences do not change that we all have the same emotions and needs. We are so much more alike than we are different—regardless of social class, race, or ethnicity.

When people see how they are "like" each other, it builds common ground and trust. It also improves our ability to communicate and relate with one another. This is called "identification theory." Identification is when your Neighbor sees how they are like you and you see how you are like them.

There are three levels of self-disclosure:
1. Sharing information only—nothing on a personal level;
2. Sharing information along with something about you that helps build common ground; and
3. Telling people your life story.

Scholar Kenneth Burke, who developed identification theory, says that you do not have to self-disclose at level three to build identification, but you do have to go to level two of self-disclosure.

- Level one does not build a connection. It is simply sharing information about a resource or building knowledge. It also includes obtaining demographics or facts about a person. Simply being in conversation with someone does not necessarily build a relationship.
- Level two shares the type of information that builds the kinds of relationships that change lives. This level simply requires individuals sharing something about yourself that builds common ground. We need to know what the other person cares about, what they value, what they dream of. Level two is also about sharing a bit of information about you—which allows them to see you as someone who is not so different from them.
- Level three is often too much sharing. It can include individuals telling each other their deepest/darkest secrets and problems. When this happens, it can make the conversation all about the speaker.

Building identification is easy. Our Neighbors need to see that you are a person like them—that you are not so different from them. You are just a person who has had different experiences and exposures than they have had. You also need to see how you are "like" your Neighbor. That is the definition of a role model: someone I can be like.

Since we are more alike than we are different, it is easy to build common ground with your fellow human beings. All humans have similar feelings. If you share what you are feeling, your Neighbor can often relate. Or, you can build common ground based on the number and/or type of siblings you have or the type of ice cream you like. Share things about your life. Tell about times when you made mistakes or felt overwhelmed. Share how you were able to overcome obstacles and times when you fell down and did not succeed. This type of sharing can build trust and improve follow-through.

Examples of this type of identification include:

- When you learn that someone was born in the same month (same state, same hospital) as you were born in.
- When you share common interests—like the same movies or music or books.
- When you share a common favorite food or dessert—maybe you have the same family traditions around a certain meal.
- When you have the same love of a certain pet—you both love dogs or cats—or even unique pets (snakes, lizards, etc.).
- Conversely, if you have the same fears (dogs, snakes, bugs)...or allergies (cats).
- When you share a common name (same middle name, mothers have the same name, etc.).
- When you share a common challenge (algebra, geometry, changing tires, etc.).

CASE STUDY

Reflecting on the case study, review and answer the following questions:

- Think about the worldviews taught by poverty. Which messages did Colleen and Jeffrey get from their parents? From their interactions at school and in the community?

- Make a list of ways to broaden possibilities for Jeffrey. How might he achieve his dream? How can you assist on his journey? Now do the same for Colleen. What can you do to assist her in gaining skills and/or an education to earn a living wage?

- Write down how you and your family are like Jeffrey and Colleen and their family.

- Make a list of what you would need to move out of poverty if you were Jeffrey or Colleen. Think about where and how you could build those resources and opportunities for this family.

Segment 5: Tools for Improving Communication and Relationships

> **Guiding Questions**
> - What are some practical ways to build trust and create relationships that matter?
> - How can I improve communication and build better relationships?
> - What are some concrete examples to improve communication, build relationships, and create welcoming environments?

Communication is complex even when we are interacting with people with similar backgrounds and life experiences. The complexities grow when we interact with those from different backgrounds and experiences. This segment will provide tools to support mutual understanding when communicating with our Neighbors who live in poverty and supply strategies for establishing trusting and productive relationships.

Building Relationships and Navigating—
Practical Ways to Build Trust and Relationships That Matter

Building a relationship with a person living in poverty can be the most impactful strategy for helping them move forward. Research on people who grew up in poverty and later became successful shows that most of them had people in their lives who helped them "navigate" the middle-class world (*Beating the Odds: How the Poor Get to College* by Levine and Nidiffer and *See Poverty…Be the Difference* by Dr. Donna M. Beegle). Moving out of poverty is not something that happens because you were "born smarter" or simply "tried harder" than others—as the Hollywood rags-to-riches movies would like you to believe. People in poverty move up when they develop meaningful, supportive relationships with individuals who help them feel like they belong and assist them in navigating the resources and opportunities needed to succeed. Below are characteristics and strategies of effective Navigators:

Believe in the person's ability to get out of poverty.

- Tell people—many times and in many ways—that you believe in them, that they are smart and can learn more, and that they have skills and talents.
- Find ways to help them understand that what they currently know is not all they can know.
- Tell stories or model ways that you built your own knowledge and developed skills to get ahead.

Believe the person has strengths and talents.
- Practice a strengths-based approach every day; look for what is good and right about people.
- Build on the person's current knowledge and skills. Suggest programs, classes, or activities that can help them move forward. When you suggest activities, tell them why you think they would be great at them.
- Set them up for success! Help them destroy barriers or navigate obstacles to attending. Make sure they have all the resources needed (transportation, clothes, etiquette, etc.) to participate in the programs you suggest.

Know the benefits of connecting people to others who are educated.
- Personally introduce people to others who are doing jobs or careers they have interest in.
- Connect people to those using education or a skill to earn a living.
- Assist people in understanding that those who are educated are not "better," they have just had different experiences and opportunities.
- Help people feel a sense of comfort and "belonging" when in new environments and with new people. As needed, help them access the supplies needed to participate; attend with them the first time; and before arriving, talk about expected rules, procedures, and etiquette.

Know that assets are critical to success and how to build them.
- Pay attention to both the internal and external capacities that your Neighbor already has—and point these out to them.
- Understand that people need supports to succeed; no one does it alone.
- Give useful information, examples, and supports to build internal capacities (self-confidence, hope) and external capacities (supplies, knowledge, transportation, etc.) for moving out and staying out of poverty. Connect the information and examples to their lived experiences.

Know how to navigate middle-class systems, procedures, and paperwork.
- Help find and connect people to the resources they need and to those who can help them.
- Assist with filling out paperwork (such as applications for services or programs, etc.).
- Teach people to advocate for themselves. Remember the mantra: Don't do it for me, do it with me.
- Role-play how to find resources and what questions to ask.
- Introduce possibilities and opportunities your Neighbor may not have considered.

Oral and Print - Two Distinct Communication and Learning Styles

Overview

Our communication style shapes how we relate and how we learn. Research reveals two distinct styles of communicating based on the ways in which people give and receive information for living their lives. Each style illuminates thought processes and learning styles. Understanding the two distinct styles can assist you in creating shared meaning and prevent misunderstandings. Understanding the two styles also has strong implications for helping people to move out and stay out of poverty.

- **Oral culture** (orality) is a natural state in which people get information for living their lives by talking to other people. They are highly attuned to senses (touch, smell, sight, sound, and taste) and devote a great deal of attention to sensory information and relationships with people.

- **Print culture** (literacy) is a learned way of relating to the world in which people often obtain information for living their lives through reading. Oral communicators become print communicators by training their brain to think in a "first this, then this" thought process. This enhances the brain's ability to analyze and classify information and develop advanced reasoning skills.

These two different ways of getting and giving information—oral and print communication styles—were first introduced by scholar Walter J. Ong (1982). According to Ong, all people are born oral culture. If they grow up in an environment where adults practice getting information for living their lives through reading, they learn to become print communicators. Oral culture does not mean that a person is illiterate; it means they prefer to get information for living their life through verbal communication.

Ong was the first to link communication styles with social class. In his worldwide research, he found that **oral**-culture communication is strongly associated with generational and working-class poverty, while **print**-culture communication is observed among families who are middle-class or higher. Specifically, he found that people living in the crisis of poverty tended to communicate more by word of mouth, while people living in an educated, middle-class context tended to obtain and give information in a more print-oriented style. Ong also discovered that people from different races and ethnicities historically tended to rely more on oral-culture styles because they had less exposure to reading for their primary information.

Both communication and learning styles have value and bring rich opportunities for human growth and connections to our world. Although one style is not better than another, in America we tend to place value on the print-culture communication, relating, and learning characteristics. In poverty and in most countries, there is more value placed on the oral-culture style of communicating, relating, and learning. The ideal is to understand the different styles and communicate in a more balanced way.

Closing the Communication Gap

Currently, the majority of U.S. institutions are set up in a way that honors, validates, and serves people with print-culture skills. Yet most people from generational poverty communicate in an oral-culture fashion. The communication gap between the social classes creates a major barrier that prevents people from building the types of relationships that can help them move out and stay out of poverty. For example, we expect people in poverty to fill out long applications, follow many steps, meet deadlines, pay attention to tasks—all print communication characteristics. Not having print communication skills is exacerbated by having to dodge the daily bullets of poverty (not having resources, responding to daily crises, etc.). When people in poverty fail to follow the print communication rules, they are often punished through denial of services and/or labeled as "not trying hard enough (being lazy)."

Outcomes of Understanding Oral and Print Styles

The benefits of practicing oral and print strategies when working with people in poverty are tremendous. They help us more effectively serve people in poverty and discover ways to help them move forward. The strategies recommended in this guide can help you:

- Suspend judgment of people who interrupt, talk loudly, and do not follow a linear schedule
- Empower people
- Ease the impact of trauma inflicted by poverty conditions
- Understand behavior
- Connect meaningfully and establish relationships
- Uncover strengths, assets, and resiliency characteristics
- Motivate people to take advantage of opportunities

1. Understanding the Characteristics of Oral and Print Communication

Walter Ong (1982) strongly emphasized that one style of communicating and learning is not better than the other. To be effective communicators, he argues, people need to have the skills from both oral and print cultures. The chart below outlines the characteristics of oral and print communications. The ideal communication style is to be balanced: having the ability to maintain both the characteristics of oral culture (which keeps one connected and spontaneous) and the characteristics of print culture (which allows one to set goals, plan ahead, analyze, and stay focused).

Characteristics of Oral Culture	Characteristics of Print Culture
• **Relationships**—People are priority and at the heart of everything. • **Spontaneous**—Strong desire for variety. Great abilities to "go with the flow" and jump from subject to subject. • **Repetitive**—Storytelling and repeating information are important for maintaining knowledge. • **Holistic**—Focus on the "BIG picture" with a tendency to take in everything that is going on around them. • **Comfortable with Emotions**—Shows emotion readily in most any situation. • **Present Oriented**—Highly in tune with the here and now. • **Agonistic**—More physical.	• **Time**—Time is at the heart of everything and has high priority in daily activities. • **Linear**—Organizes thoughts and actions by a "first this, then this" process. • **Analytic/Abstract**—Knowledge is outside of self; ability to step back from a situation and separate and disconnect oneself from what is going on. • **Self-Disciplined/Focused**—Strong ability to shut out sensory data and focus on one idea at a time. • **Strategic**—Ability to plan ahead, set goals, and focus on the future. • **Delay Gratification**—Ability to break things into parts, which promotes the ability to connect small efforts to the desired outcomes.

2. Practicing a Balanced Style of Communicating

Many people who are print-culture communicators lose touch with their natural style of communicating. They often become so dominant in print culture that they struggle to retain many of the characteristics that oral-culture people exhibit readily, such as the ability to develop relationships and be "in the moment." Likewise, people who are steeped in oral culture struggle with print-culture characteristics, such as breaking things into manageable steps or planning ahead. Poverty compounds this because they often plan ahead and then do not have the resources to follow through or a crisis happens that interrupts their plans. A balanced communicator will skillfully use characteristics of each style as appropriate for communicating most effectively. To become more balanced, practice the strengths of your less dominant communication style.

To practice more ORAL skills	To practice more PRINT skills
• Follow your intuition and act on it. • Pay attention to your feelings and tell others how you feel about them. • Be more of a listener than a speaker. Practice active listening to stay in the moment and to build better relationships. • Practice empathy to gain insights into how you are like others. • Respond immediately without thinking. • Stay focused on the moment. • Sing, dance, and be silly! • Pay attention to your environment. • Put people first—ask about the person before talking about the agenda.	• Practice reading as a primary source for gaining important daily life information. • Create lists. Practice sorting and categorizing. • Outline key points from the concepts and discussions. • Break tasks into explicit, small steps that are specific and manageable. • Seek examples of completed work as models to follow. • Write your life story to practice recording information. • Use a calendar and address book to keep track of dates and contact information.

3. Honoring Oral Communication Style

There is a dominant belief in the United States that the oral-culture style of communicating is inferior and requires less intelligence. However, there is evidence that oral culture has its own unique strengths. Many of the cultures that have been ecologically sustainable over hundreds or thousands of years are oral cultures. Many of the characteristics of these oral cultures are characteristics found in societies that live within the ability of the earth to replenish itself, such as:

- Emphasis on relationships
- Respect of the limitation of resources of the earth
- Closer connection to the earth and its cycles
- Less focus on material possessions
- In flow with relationships and time

Too often, oral communicators feel "punished" for their style of communicating. Think about the student who gets in trouble for not raising their hand to speak in class, the client who misses an important legal meeting because they didn't read the mailed notice—rather relying on getting important information verbally—or the co-worker who shares too much private information with colleagues and becomes a social outcast. Punishing people for their oral style of communicating is a way of devaluing them. However, when people feel valued, they are more engaged and productive. We improve outcomes when we see the strengths in oral communicators, while teaching them the print skills they need to be successful.

Strategies to Honor Oral Culture

- Develop relationships based on identification. Oral-culture communicators learn best from someone they feel connected to. Find ways to show that you have commonalities.
- Tell stories. Use vivid examples that draw people in and get their attention.
- Use simple, familiar words and examples that people can relate to.
- Give information verbally—often, repeatedly, and with good eye contact.
- Help oral-culture learners feel confident. Research shows that self-confidence affects the ability to remember. Help them focus on what they have done well, rather than their mistakes.
- Share information in multiple ways. Help oral-culture learners hear the information—write it, see it, and practice it. Learning something new in multiple ways helps with recalling information.
- Use gestures and facial expressions when communicating.

4. Teaching Print Skills

Assisting our oral-culture Neighbors to gain the skill sets of print culture is important for moving out of poverty. It is the dominant style used in the workplace and in education. Effective communication cannot be achieved without educating all people on ways to broaden their repertoire and develop their less dominant style of learning and communicating. Below are some strategies for teaching print skills to those you serve.

Strategies to Teach Print Culture

- Model reading as a way to get useful information, such as helping people to research information in a book or on the internet.
- Create template sheets of paper that have numbered lines and work with your Neighbor to break actions into small, doable steps.
- Practice linear thinking. Work with your Neighbor to make a "first this, then this" list of things to do.
- Use mnemonic devices. Have people imagine an image of what you want them to remember. If it is a date or name, give an image to associate it with. For example, "My name is Donna Beegle, like the dog, but with two 'e's.'"
- Short sayings that tell a story are also helpful to create print-culture skills sets. For example, "If you're not 15 minutes early, you're late." (Of course, you would not expect people to be early or even on time if they are in crisis.)

ACTIVITY

What Is Your Dominant Communication Style?

The tool on the next page can assist you in exploring your dominant style of communication. It can also provide you with insights for developing strategies to better connect with and serve those you work with.

Instructions: Read each statement on the chart and write your score in the box to the right of the statement. Rate each statement on a scale of 1-5 depending on how much the statement describes your behavior.

1. No. This statement does not describe my style.
2. Mostly Not. This statement is mostly not true for me.
3. Sometimes. Half the time, this statement is true for me.
4. Mostly Yes. This statement captures my style most of the time.
5. Yes. This statement describes my style.

Add the score in each column. If the two totals are close to the same number, congratulations! Walter Ong would say you are a balanced communicator. This allows you to use the skill sets of each style to respond appropriately in any given situation. If you have a 20 percent higher score in either oral or print communication, examine how you can gain and implement the skills to achieve balance for communicating and relating more effectively.

- If you scored higher on oral and lower on print, read the print strategies on page 41 and begin incorporating them into your communication and daily activities.
- If you scored higher on print and lower on oral, read the oral strategies on page 40 and begin incorporating them into your communication and daily activities.

ACTIVITY
What Is Your Dominant Communication Style?

Creating a welcoming environment is a priority. I set the tone by noticing people and learning their names and interests.		I like to focus on ideas and agendas—usually focusing on one item at a time.	
Relationships are more important than rules or procedures. I put people first.		I prefer rules to ambiguity.	
I like to have multiple conversations at once.		I do not interrupt.	
I learn best from telling or listening to stories.		I want just facts, not stories.	
I like to work in groups, socialize, and learn from other people, even though it may be noisy from conversations.		I prefer to work quietly—alone or one-on-one.	
I prefer conversations about people.		I prefer conversations about ideas.	
In conversations, I pay attention to facial expressions, body posture, and tone of voice more than the content of what is being said.		In conversations, I focus on the content of what's being said more than the nonverbals and the environment in which it is being said.	
I have a schedule but change it according to the situation.		Time is crucial and I am rigid about it.	
I like frequent reminders.		I believe a plan is essential and my goal is to stay on task.	
I like to touch, try, and experiment when I am learning.		I approach work by breaking tasks into clear steps.	
When I need information for living my life, I'll ask someone I trust—someone who is like me.		When I need information for living my life, I'll research it and read the information.	
I am physical and expect physical responses.		I only show emotions and share feelings with people I know really well.	
I tell everyone just about everything! That's the only way they will really know me.		I do not share personal stories.	
	Oral Total		**Print Total**

www.combarriers.com   Communication Across Barriers

10 Strategies to Communicate and Build Relationships That Matter

1. Be aware of your own bias, including internal feelings of discomfort around differences. It will show in your nonverbals (tone of voice, facial expressions, and body posture). Use genuine, welcoming facial expressions, a warm tone of voice, and positive body language. With this awareness, you are more empowered to suspend judgment and share information to assist Neighbors with resources and opportunities for moving out of poverty.

2. Increase follow-through by disclosing something about yourself and allowing Neighbors to see you as a real person with whom they can identify. Personal connection will go a long way toward showing your Neighbor that you are a real human being who cares about them.

3. Ensure the messages you send are the messages being heard: Paraphrase, restate with a variety of different examples, ask clarifying questions, and ask the Neighbor what they heard you say.

4. Avoid focusing solely on the problems or task at hand (providing food, clothing, rent assistance, etc.). Listen closely to understand what they wish could happen and what is in their way. Make an effort to compliment something the Neighbor displays that can be a talent or skill—something that the Neighbor could use to help solve their own problem.

5. Use visuals as much as possible to accommodate oral-culture communication styles (including drawing out next steps, using bullet points, and using stories as a way to communicate information).

6. Breaking barriers requires accessing both resources and opportunities to move forward. Don't expect people to know what may be obvious to you or to feel comfortable doing something that seems commonplace to you. Use your expertise to coach and navigate people to resources and opportunities.

7. Use active listening techniques, such as suspending your thoughts about what you are going to say in response to the client. Avoid focusing on non-related subjects. Repeat back—every so often—what you hear to make sure you are understanding correctly and comprehending the other person's perspective, explanations, and rationale.

8. There are many lived experiences of poverty, so one solution will not work for everyone. Obtain enough information from the Neighbor and their circumstances to customize your services and be flexible in response to their choices of desired next steps.

9. Promote two-way communication (not only what you think would work for Neighbors, but what they think would work best for them).

10. Ask open-ended questions to understand Neighbors' perspectives and try to stay away from questions that ask "why," because they can put people on the defense. Instead, use statements such as, "Help me understand" or "Tell me a little more about..."

CASE STUDY

Reflecting on the case study, review and answer the following questions:

- Below are best practices for mentoring and navigating people out of poverty. Reflect on the characteristics of effective Navigators. Determine how you might use these to help build a relationship with Jeffrey and Colleen. What could you say to Jeffrey/Colleen about each of these points?

    - Believe in the person's ability to get out of poverty.

    - Believe in and highlight the person's strengths and talents.

    - Suspend judgment and give people the benefit of the doubt. Assume they are doing the best they can with what they have been exposed to and the situation they are in.

    - Connect your Neighbors to people who are not living in the crisis of poverty. They need to build their address books with people who earn a living wage and know how to navigate resources and opportunities.

- Review the 10 Strategies to Communicate and Build Relationships That Matter (from the previous page). Pick one or two of them and write how you could use them to communicate and relate more effectively with Jeffrey and/or Colleen.

Segment 6: Call to Action, Call to Hope

> **Guiding Questions**
> - What actions can we take to work together to build the kind of community where everyone thrives?
> - How do we build organizations that go beyond helping people to cope with poverty?
> - What tools can each of us use to create solutions and assist our Neighbors to move out and stay out of poverty?

For far too long, efforts to address poverty have—at best—helped people to cope with their poverty. Organizations in our community often work in isolation and address a single poverty barrier ("Here's a three-day box of food; good luck"). This is helpful but not effective in assisting our Neighbors to move out of poverty. The thought behind these efforts is that—with a little bit of help—people will get back on their feet. The problem is many of our Neighbors have no stable place to live and some never have a home to call their own. Others do not have the skills or education to earn a living wage. They are often working but unable to make ends meet or pay for the additional education and skills needed to succeed.

Improving outcomes for our Neighbors means creating organizations that are poverty informed and work with others in the community to remove obstacles. Providing a comprehensive approach requires systemic change. Research on organizational change has shown that sustainable change must come from within and must be grounded in the community's vision and leadership capacity (Schein, 1992; Fullan, 2001). Each community—rural or urban—has its own strengths and assets to call upon. Because single-focused approaches do not work to move people out of poverty, we all need to come together and offer resources and opportunities.

Examining our organizations through a poverty-informed lens leads to systemic change. Are our policies working to empower people living in crisis? Do the people within our organizations believe people can make it out of poverty? Do we have strong partnerships to address the complexities of poverty? Systemic change happens when people become aware of and challenge practices that are not centered on assisting people to move out and stay out of poverty. There is no quick fix to make an organization responsive and successful in addressing the needs of people in poverty. Rather, it is an evolutionary process that can lead an organization to partner and collaborate in ways that change lives.

In this session, we will explore proven models and strategies for working together in a poverty-informed, connected approach. We will discuss how to tap into existing resources to build pathways out of poverty.

What Can You Do?

- **Continue Learning About Poverty and Its Impacts.** Poverty requires ongoing examination, knowledge gathering, and listening to those impacted.

- **Use the Strategies Taught by Dr. Beegle.** In spite of the lack of education in our country about poverty, there are research-based strategies for assisting Neighbors in breaking the cycle of poverty. Pages 19-20 summarizes five theories and provides strategies you can apply.

- **Operate Like NASA**: Failure Is Not an Option. If you cannot connect with those you serve or resolve a poverty issue, who in your network or community might be able to? Use an "If not me, then who?" approach.

- **Collaborate and Strengthen Partnerships.** Poverty is complex and requires a comprehensive, community-wide approach. Connect with health providers, social workers, retirement communities, justice professionals, educators, faith-based organizations, and others. Explore the skills and resources they offer that may assist you in breaking poverty barriers. Create a "full resource backpack"—an inventory of who in your community may be able to assist individuals with ending the cycle, gaining stability, and moving out of poverty.

- **Be a Thought Leader in Your Community.** We graduate people from college without Poverty 101. Our endeavors to assist our Neighbors must include efforts to educate and raise awareness in your community. Do brown bag lunches and go through the Beegle Poverty Awareness videos and materials with community partners. Together, a poverty-informed collective can create communities where eliminating poverty is a main objective.

- **Always Work with Your Neighbor.** "Do not do it for me, do it with me." Listen carefully to your Neighbor's dreams and what is in their way before working on an action plan WITH them.

Research shows that individuals experiencing poverty may need assistance in the following areas:

1. **Removing the shame** that prevents the person from moving forward. Help your Neighbor see they are not the cause of poverty.

2. **Rebuilding the hope** that stops someone from taking opportunities that are offered. You can build hope by assisting your Neighbor in seeing that they already know some things that can be used on their journey to earn a living. When people see they are not stupid or deficient and when they are exposed to possibilities with doable steps, hope returns.

3. **Reducing the isolation** of poverty by connecting your Neighbor to Navigators/mentors who are poverty informed and who will walk with them on their journey to move out and stay out of poverty.

4. **Creating a poverty-informed community**. Serve as an advocate when your Neighbor interacts with community organizations. Share your poverty-informed perspectives and ensure your community is fighting the poverty, not the people who are in it.

Strategies to Remove Shame

Point out that your Neighbor is not alone in their struggles. There are 43 million people facing the impacts of poverty: lights being shut off, cars being towed, families being evicted from their homes, children not having enough to eat, and many more!

Talk about the real causes of poverty: lack of affordable housing, lack of living-wage jobs, limited access to excellent child care and schools, limited access to nutrition and preventive care, etc. Your goal is to assure them that their personality and choices are not the cause of their poverty. There are real, structural causes.

Have Neighbors make a list of everything they do in one day. Pull actions from their lists and link them to professional jobs that pay a living wage. Show them how much those professions pay and then break down what is in their way to begin the journey toward the life they want. For instance:

- You manage money when you have it; you could be an accountant.
- You are good at throwing parties; you could be an event planner.
- You are a great listener; you could be a counselor.
- You like to argue; you could be an attorney.

Strategies to Rebuild Hope

Hope is the wings for grabbing opportunity. The four biggest sources for rebuilding hope are:

- Learning that the people who are making it are not better than you are. Rather, they are people who had exposure to different opportunities.
- Learning that you are not stupid. You know some things that could lead to earning a living.
- Achieving small daily successes toward your dreams.
- Learning that your fellow human beings care about you and that you do not have to try to fight the complexities of poverty alone.

Examples of caring behavior:

- One of the most powerful messages that poverty teaches is that no one cares. Show people you care by learning their name. Find out what is important to them and ask about their dreams for themselves and their children.
- Humans are drawn to others who share similar life experiences and values. Share information about yourself at level two self-disclosure so Neighbors can see you are just a person who is not so different from them.
- Give useful information and resources that alleviate the impacts of poverty.
- Do not judge! Seek to understand the "why" behind the behavior. There is always a "why" that makes sense if you contextualize the behavior and hear it from the other person's perspective.
- Help Neighbors shift their thinking toward possibilities. Share real, doable ideas for moving out of poverty.

Strategies to Reduce Isolation

Connect Neighbors to Navigators/mentors who will make a commitment to walking with them on their journey to move out and stay out of poverty.

Characteristics to effectively mentor Neighbors out of poverty:

1. Believe in their unlimited potential. What they know when you meet them is not all they can know.
2. Assist Neighbors to see the strengths and skills that they already have.
3. Get poverty informed. If you are judging, you cannot connect. If you cannot

connect, you cannot communicate. If you cannot communicate, you will not make a difference.

4. Introduce Neighbors to others who can provide resources and opportunities. Build their address books with as many people who are not in the crisis of poverty as they have in their lives who are struggling.

Host potlucks and events that bring your community together. Assign individuals to ensure that Neighbors are introduced to and interacting with others who can build relationships across social class barriers.

Teach networking skills. Role-play informational interviews in fields the Neighbor is interested in. Help them to set up three 15-minute interviews to learn how people got into their professions. Encourage Neighbors to send thank-you notes (one every two months for six months) sharing what they are doing to move toward that career/job. Provide access to thank-you cards, envelopes, and stamps.

Strategies for Creating a Poverty-Informed Community

A few ways to create a poverty-informed community include:

- Staff and community members gain knowledge and skills regarding poverty.
- Poverty competency issues and barriers to information and services are openly discussed in meetings and within the organization and community.
- Staff and community members "walk the talk" of collaboration. They are familiar with local poverty-fighting organizations as well as organizations that can provide opportunities to people living in the crisis of poverty. A conscious effort is made to link people to resources and opportunities.
- Staff and community members are conscious about how different experiences, perceptions, and communication styles affect priorities and relationships. Perspectives and goals of people living in poverty are heard before sharing possible solutions.
- Staff and community members are aware of their own perceptions about difference and are able to suspend judgment of behavior, attitude, and styles that may not match their own.
- Organizational policies and procedures are flexible enough to work for everyone, not just those with economic privilege.

- Staff members spend time sharing "what worked and what could have been better" for assisting people to break down poverty-related barriers.
- Staff and community members recognize people fighting poverty also have knowledge and skills that can be tapped into to help them move out of poverty.

In conversations with peers and community and/or family members, you might run up against some challenges. As an advocate, you should expect that stereotypes will be brought up in these conversations because the majority of your community has only been informed about poverty through the media. Don't take offense and don't get upset. If you do, you won't be heard. (The statement about if you judge, you cannot connect, etc., is also true when speaking with community members!)

To make an impact, build your resource backpack.

1. Ask professionals in your community to tell you more about what they do and how you can assist Neighbors in accessing the resources and opportunities they offer.
2. Research poverty in your community and share the facts. Stay informed, so you will be able to reframe judgment and blame with facts.
3. Share real stories of the obstacles your Neighbors are facing. Poverty, not people, is the problem.

CASE STUDY

Reflecting on the case study, review and write about the following ideas:

- There are three specific areas where people experiencing poverty need assistance. Take a few minutes to determine how you could help Jeffrey and Colleen and their children in each of these areas.

    - Removing the Shame

    - Rebuilding the Hope

    - Reducing the Isolation

Segment 7: Digging Deeper

Guiding Questions

- What are the best strategies for creating systemic change?
- How can we lead and create an Opportunity Community?

> *"Systemic change does not miraculously bubble up from a change of heart. It is intentional, stemming from a precise and rigorous examination of present conditions and an understanding of the consciousness and spirit from which those conditions have emerged."*
>
> —Dr. Sharif Abdullah

Systemic Change

Systemic change is not easy, nor does it happen overnight—but it does happen. In the 1900s, it was difficult for girls and women to succeed in the American education system. Commentators said that the education system was like the Titanic and impossible to change. However, today, more women receive college degrees than men. What happened? What did we do in our education system that made it possible for girls and women to succeed today? It began with systemic changes in our organizations. We began looking at the policies in our educational system and questioning: Do these policies serve girls and women and set them up for success? Anti-discrimination policies were then passed at the federal level that forced educational policy changes. School board members and education leaders were forced to examine their attitudes, beliefs, and values about whether they believed females should be educated in order to remain in compliance with federal mandates. School districts began reviewing the relevancy of education curriculum to ensure more success for girls and women. Education leaders adopted school-wide gender-based anti-discrimination policies and offered gender diversity trainings to teachers and staff.

To develop systems that better serve people living in poverty, we must begin by becoming poverty informed and capturing a snapshot of how the current system is working. We have to determine what most organizations have been doing to eradicate poverty and explore if it has been working.

Individuals and organizations working with people in poverty must actively apply change theory. This first requires examining individual attitudes, beliefs, and values as well as organizational cultures and norms. Each organization must problem-solve, understand, and create their own plans and interventions to respond to the needs of people living in poverty in their community. What we need is to transform our organizational cultures into those that embrace and empower people from poverty to overcome the barriers to success.

Single-Focus Approach

"Success flows not from any single approach or silver bullet but from millions upon millions of individual face-to-face actions and transactions. Success is marked by the rebirth of hope, opportunity and freedom—hope for a better life, free from want, free from disease, free from fear." —President Kennedy, inaugural address (1960)

Some social problems are well defined and the solutions are clear. For those problems, a single-focused approach by one or a few agencies may work. This is the typical approach to addressing poverty, which is fragmented and normally only addresses a single aspect of poverty, such as:

1. clothing
2. education
3. employment
4. food
5. health care, emergency room care, mental health care, hospice, home health
6. housing

One major problem with single-focus approaches is a lack of emphasis on the desired outcomes. For instance, when the desired outcome is to end hunger, providing a three-day box of emergency food will take care of the family for three days but will not end their hunger for the remainder of the year. Giving a person a box of food or a voucher for something they need may help them cope for the day, but it does not help them move out and stay out of poverty.

Most poverty problems are complex and no one organization has the resources or authority to adequately address these issues. Isolated interventions rarely produce the solutions to the multifaceted poverty issues. In order to solve these complex and interdependent problems, it requires learning by the stakeholders involved in the problem who must change their own behavior in order to create a solution. It requires a systemic approach that focuses on the relationships between organizations and their progress toward shared objectives.

The Opportunity Community Model

Dr. Beegle's Opportunity Community (OC) Model is a national movement designed to create the types of communities we all want to live in—communities where all members thrive and are connected to one another. The OC Model uses a connected/comprehensive, people-to-people approach for assisting people in moving out and staying out of the war zone of poverty. The core principles that guide the model are:

1. Remove the shame that prevents our Neighbors from seeing and taking opportunities

2. Rebuild the hope for both people in poverty and those wanting to make a real difference

3. Reducing the isolation that perpetuates poverty by connecting people in poverty to people who are not in poverty (poverty-informed Navigators).

4. Build a responsive, poverty-informed community by providing structured ways for community members to understand poverty and to become active and engaged in improving outcomes for their Neighbors in poverty

5. Assist people in obtaining skills and/or education necessary to earn a living

The OC Model employs a comprehensive approach that builds on the existing strengths of people in business, social service, education, health care, justice, faith-based organizations, and community members—along with the strengths of the people in poverty—to make a difference for their community. This model has components for engaging diverse support from the community; however, the OC Model goes beyond building collaborations and partnerships.

At its core, the OC Model:

1. Serves people from generational, working-class, situational, mixed-class, and immigrant poverty
2. Provides structure for a better-connected community network resulting in a more effective and efficient poverty-fighting system
3. Provides community-wide education to increase awareness and understanding about the real causes of poverty—educating people living in poverty (Neighbors) and volunteers (Navigators and Specialty Navigators), then connecting Navigators and Neighbors in strong relationships
4. Trains community professionals to serve as specialty Navigators and support the efforts of Navigators who are working to access resources and opportunities for their Neighbors
5. Increases engagement of sectors of the community not previously involved in fighting poverty
6. Builds capacity of helping professionals who serve people in poverty

Results of Being an Opportunity Community:

- **Better-Connected Community**—across ages, races, incomes, and education levels.

- **Strengthened Social Safety Net**—new resources, more people engaged in fighting poverty, and enhanced use of existing resources.

- **Trained Navigators and Specialty Navigators**—increase in community members active and engaged in bettering their community.

- **Empowered Neighbors**—low-income individuals and families with hope, tools, support, and connections to get out and stay out of poverty. The ability to use new tools and ideas as well as better awareness of the resources that are already available. An understanding that they are cared about by their community. (Specific comments from a few Neighbors on next page.)

"I did not know my community cared about me. I was homeless when I came to the conference. When the Navigators came in and said they would give us their personal phone number and call to help, I was shocked and did not believe it. One year later, with the help of my Navigator, I had my own apartment, furniture, and my dream job of working as a music and sound professional."

—*50-year-old male*

"I went to Neighbor Connection because I did not know what else to do. I was in an abusive relationship and had no hope for getting out. My clothes were ragged; my children had no beds and ragged clothes. I decided that my only choice was for me to take the lives of my children and my life. One year after the Neighbor Connection, I am out of the abusive situation. I feel hope, I smile, and with the help of my Navigator, I am in college learning English. My children see a good future."

—*25-year-old female*

"I came to Neighbor Connection because my girlfriend was going. I had an infection in my jawbone and only seven teeth. No one wanted to hire me because of my hygiene and I only had a high school education. I can honestly say, I learned a lot and, for the first time, believed that I had something to offer the world. I was matched with a Navigator who helped me get my teeth fixed. I can smile now and I am looking for work with confidence."

—*22-year-old male*

"I was homeless with my three-year-old daughter. Everyone always told me I was stupid and retarded and I could not learn. I was amazed to learn at Neighbor Connection about different ways people learn. That made so much sense to me. A year later, I have an apartment and I am working on my G.E.D. I learned people do care and I am not alone."

—*18-year-old female*

CASE STUDY

Reflecting on the case study, review and answer the following questions:

- Discuss your ideas for what a comprehensive approach to help Jeffrey and his family might look like in your community. What stakeholders need to be involved? What knowledge or skills do you have that might be helpful? How might you connect the family to the other resources and opportunities that can help them reach their dreams?

Next Steps

Congratulations on completing the Beegle poverty awareness training. We hope that this is not the end but that new doors open to continue your work as thought leaders and life changers.

Dr. Beegle Recommends These Next Steps:

1. Next-Level Professional Development Sessions: Breaking poverty barriers requires ongoing learning. Dr. Beegle will work with you to identify target areas for growth and customize next-level trainings to meet those objectives.

2. Video Training and Book Reads: *See Poverty...Be the Difference* and *An Action Approach to Educating Students in Poverty* assist participants in taking the learning to a deeper level. *An Action Approach* comes with a two-hour, five-topic training DVD and companion *Action Approach Guidebook* for applying Dr. Beegle's concepts and seeing measurable results. Both are available at www.combarriers.com.

See Poverty...Be the Difference. This resource provides an authentic opportunity for gaining a foundation, rooted in lived experience and research, for understanding poverty and addressing its impacts. It is designed to shatter stereotypes with facts and to provide concrete tools and ideas for creating programs and systems that are responsive to the needs of people living in poverty.

An Action Approach to Educating Students in Poverty, focusing on educators, comes with a 2-hour, 5-topic training DVD and companion Action Approach Guidebook for applying Dr. Beegle's concepts and seeing measurable results. In this groundbreaking training dvd, participants gain practical strategies from an insider perspective on how we can improve educational outcomes for students who live in poverty.

Breaking Poverty Barriers to Equal Justice. This highly interactive training will equip legal professionals with practical tools for improving services. The 5-session training video and companion guidebook are designed to increase awareness of poverty and its profound impacts on the people served. Using in-depth analysis of different life experiences of poverty and how each impacts access to legal services, legal professionals will gain a foundational knowledge for addressing short- and long-term poverty obstacles to equal justice. The book provides hands-on activities and real-world case studies to increase the ability to communicate and relate more effectively with people experiencing the impacts of poverty.

3. Send a Team to Attend the Beegle Poverty Institute: The intensive two-day Poverty Institute provides a grounded understanding of poverty and concrete tools for breaking poverty barriers to success. The Poverty Institute is designed for professionals from the fields of justice, education, health, and social service, as well as faith-based, business, and community organization members.

4. Send a Team to Become Beegle Certified Poverty Coaches: The intensive two-day Beegle Poverty Coaching Institute prepares participants for leading systemic change within their organizations. Participants gain skills for providing ongoing poverty competencies, teaching professional development workshops, conducting poverty competency assessments, and developing measurable action plans for improving outcomes. Register at www.combarriers.com.

5. Partner with Our Team: Host the Beegle Poverty Institute and Poverty Coaching Institute in your community. Contact Elia Moreno, national program director, at elia@combarriers.com for more information.

6. Become an Opportunity Community: Dr. Beegle has researched best practices, nationally and internationally, that work to improve outcomes for children and families living in the crisis of poverty. Out of this research, Dr. Beegle developed the Opportunity Community (OC) model. The OC model is a community-wide approach that includes programs for students and families who currently live in poverty. The pillars of the model are to: 1) Remove the shame and judgment; 2) Rebuild the hope; 3) Reduce the isolation; and 4) Create a poverty-informed community that works together to improve outcomes. Communities can work to implement the proven best practices on their own or contact Dr. Beegle's organization for implementation of the full model. For more information on how you can become an Opportunity Community, contact our national program director, Elia Moreno, at elia@combarriers.com.

7. Bring a Communication Across Barriers Team Member in for a Poverty Competency Assessment (PCA): Dr. Beegle developed the Poverty Competency Assessment and action planning tools to create more responsive systems. The PCA examines all aspects of the organization to identify areas that are meeting or exceeding desired outcomes and how to do more of what works. It illuminates areas for growth (where we keep doing what we have always done even though we are not achieving desired outcomes). The process identifies professional development levels of staff for addressing poverty barriers. It also captures the strengths of partnerships necessary for providing a comprehensive approach to removing poverty barriers. Programs, curricula, and communication and teaching styles are also captured to ensure we are communicating and providing information in relevant, meaningful ways. The PCA results in a Poverty Competency Plan with measurable, doable actions. The Poverty Competency Plan can be incorporated into organizational strategic plans. For more information, contact our office at 503-590-4599.

8. Partner with CAB and Dr. Beegle to Develop a Custom Training DVD and Materials for Your Organization.

"Dr. Donna Beegle's poverty work and Poverty Coach Certification are the foundation of our new approach to serving students. These trainings have completely changed our understanding of who our students are and what they need from us. The Poverty and Coaching Institutes will be the best professional development investment in your employees and organization you could possibly experience. The interactive experience will change your hearts, challenge your minds and improve your impact, personally and organizationally."

—Dr. Russell Lowery-Hart, President, Amarillo College

Post-Training Reflection

Now that you have been through the seven segments of this training, please take a few minutes to reflect on the following questions and write down your answers as completely and thoughtfully as possible. Review the answers you wrote in your Pre-Training Reflection and reflect on how they have changed.

1. When you hear the word *poverty*, what are the first images and words that come to your mind? How has your definition of poverty changed?

2. What causes poverty?

3. What actions are needed to improve outcomes for Neighbors living in the crisis of poverty?

4. Based on your past interactions with your Neighbors in poverty, how were your experiences and exposure to opportunities—while growing up—similar to or different from those of the people struggling in poverty whom you want to empower?

5. Are you able to suspend judgment and believe that people are making the best decisions possible from their perspective? How?